Little Flowers on the Prairie
by Cathy Smith, Overland Park, Kan.
59"x 59"

A Heartland Album

More Techniques in Hand Appliqué

By Kathy Delaney

KANSAS CITY STAR BOOKS

ACKNOWLEDGEMENTS

Without the support of family and friends, very few of us could accomplish anything major. We all start from within, but then we need help from others to keep us going. Their encouragement, inspiration and sometimes nagging help the process immeasurably.

A big thank you goes to Rich, Sean and Ian Delaney and to Vi Berry (my family) for their encouragement, support and grounding. You have to admit that I've been much better about the pins!

Thank you, too, to Doug Weaver for giving me yet another opportunity to share my passion with you all. Thank you to Judy Pearlstein, the editor; Vicky Frenkel, the designer; Bill Krzyzanowski, the photographer; and Jo Ann Groves at the Kansas City Star for making this book beautiful. Thank you to Tresa Jones and her family for the use of antiques and personal possessions for the studio photographs. Thanks to Mary Agnew and Pam Crain for the use of your treasures, too. And thank you to Leanne Baraban and Susan Winnie for giving their time to help with the instructional photographs.

I am constantly learning from my students. I want to thank each and every one of you for your insights,

support and encouragement. It is for you that I write this book. Your passion for quilting and learning about quilting are what make me want to share what I know.

My "Quilt Sisters," Leanne Baraban, Charlotte Gurwell and Linda Potter, keep me grounded and keep me dreaming at the same time. Without you I don't think I would have the courage to attempt this book writing stuff! Thank you for believing in me.

A huge thank you goes to the ladies who were inspired by my patterns to use them in projects of their own for the gallery of this book. Thank you Kathy Berner, Donna Howard, Tresa Jones, Carol Kirchhoff, Linda Mooney, Pat Moore, Nancy Nunn, Michelle Sieben, Cathy Smith, Dorothy Stalling and Geraldine Strader.

And I want to thank you, the reader, for showing your faith in me by buying this book. I hope that it provides lots of inspiration for you for adding texture to your quilted projects. May your quilts and life be full of texture!

A Heartland Album
Author: Kathy Delaney

Editor: Judy Pearlstein
Designer: Vicky Frenkel
Photography: Bill Krzyzanowski
Antiques provided by Tresa Jones, Mary Agnew and Pam Crain
Instructional photographs by Kathy Delaney with
Leanne Baraban and Susan Winnie

Published by:
Kansas City Star Books
1729 Grand Blvd.
Kansas City, Missouri, USA 64108

First edition

Library of Congress Card Number:2003102203

ISBN 0-9722739-7-2

Printed in the United States of America by Walsworth Publishing Co., Marceline, MO

To order copies, call StarInfo at (816) 234-4636 and say "Books."
Or go to www.PickleDish.com

Kansas City Star Quilts

TABLE OF CONTENTS

Whispers
by Kathy Delaney, Overland Park, Kan.
quilted by Jeanne Zyck
62"x 62"

About the Author

Kathy Delaney, who has a degree in art education from the University of Arizona, loves to teach. Beginning with teaching art to elementary children and high school children, she soon graduated to adults, teaching needlepoint and then quilting techniques. She has been working and teaching at Prairie Point Quilts in Shawnee, Kansas, since it opened in June 1995.

An award-winning quilter, Kathy's work has been published in several books, magazines and a calendar.

The technique that brings Kathy the most satisfaction is needleturn appliqué and her greatest joy is teaching appliqué to those who always insisted that they would never do the "A" Word!

Kathy lives in Overland Park, Kansas, with her husband of 31 years. Together they have two sons: Sean, a Second Lieutenant in the U.S. Army, and Ian, a freshman at the University of Arizona, majoring in Theatre Performing Arts.

Kathy designs patterns for piecing and appliqué under the name of Fabric Crayon Designs.

Introduction

A HEARTLAND ALBUM – MORE TECHNIQUES IN HAND APPLIQUÉ

If I've said it once, I've said hundreds of times: *Appliqué is painting with fabric.* And I love to paint!

When I was in high school, I had the opportunity to work in a variety of mediums that I'd never used before and I painted my first oil painting. The colors were vibrant and exciting but the surface was flat. Something seemed to be missing. When I went to art school and college, I discovered various brushes and the pallet knife and what they could do. The colors were still vibrant and exciting but the surface of my paintings began to take on texture: texture from the brush and my strokes and texture from the application of paint using the pallet knife.

Now that you have mastered the hand appliqué techniques found in *Hearts and Flowers – Hand Appliqué from Start to Finish*, you might like to add some texture to your appliqué work with the techniques you'll find within these pages. I designed my *Prairie Album* to use many

techniques that would surely add texture.

For every appliqué artist, you'll find that there is at least one system, if not several, to accomplish the techniques used. I have tried every technique I've met and modified them to suit me. In this book I will show you what I do. This is not to say that what I do is the only way to do any of the techniques. I have just found that what I'm showing you here is the easiest for *me*. I hope that you will be inspired and that you find the techniques easy for you.

Besides the traditional needles, threads and scissors for appliqué, dimensional appliqué utilizes a variety of tools and gadgets. I will give you the information on how I use them. Please note that the designers of the tools and gadgets may have had other ideas of how to use their tools and it is worth investigating their ideas. Their directions will usually come with the tool or gadget at the point of purchase. For your convenience, after the last chapter I will include a resource list so that if your favorite quilting supply store does not carry the item, you will know how to contact someone to obtain your own.

Besides texture, I am going to introduce you to some techniques that are considered "advanced." If you take it just one stitch at a time, however, I really think you'll find that the so-called advanced techniques aren't any more difficult than the needleturn appliqué you accomplished with your own *Hearts and Flowers* quilt.

I trust that the Gallery will inspire you. Please notice that there are lots of projects that you can accomplish with appliqué patterns that aren't exactly appliqué. I have tried to include a variety of techniques in this book that use the *Prairie Album* patterns but aren't all appliqué. So have some fun! There are no limits!

When I created my *Prairie Album*, I put myself in the shoes of one who had been transplanted from someplace else (I had recently moved from Michigan) to the prairie of Kansas (where I now live). I tried to imagine some of the symbols that I might have left behind (such as the pineapple depicting "Welcome"), some of the plants I might have come across on the prairie ("Hot Poker Vine" and "Prairie Flower") and some of the familiar designs I might have used often before ("Open Bud-Wreath"). I chose fabrics that would speak more of the country than the city. But think of the possibilities! With the same patterns, you could create a whimsical quilt with the bright prints that are so popular right now, or something totally different by using some of Robyn Pandolf's soft pastel fabrics designed for Moda, or how about the intriguing patterns found in batik prints from the South Seas? You are only limited by your imagination!

Chapter One

NEEDLETURN APPLIQUÉ REVIEWED

FABRICS

Appliqué can be accomplished with almost any fabric. Each fabric will present its own set of guidelines and challenges. For our purposes, however, unless specifically noted, assume that all the fabrics used in all of the quilts and projects depicted in this book are 100% natural cotton, quilt shop quality. Needleturn appliqué is most easily accomplished with cotton, whether it is homespun, flannel, or printed muslin weight. And even though I'm going to introduce you to more techniques in this book, ultimately, my work begins with needleturn appliqué.

When choosing fabric for my projects, I often look for an "inner light." I look for a variation in values and visual textures as well as movement created by the print design. Often, I enjoy using hand dyed fabrics as they hold some very interesting color play and can offer me subtle shading. However, I have also noticed that the hand dyes don't always seem to contribute much. If an appliqué shape is rather small, the fabric reads as a solid because the shading happens so gradually. I save my hand dyed fabrics for larger pieces and backgrounds. Cotton batiks are also visually exciting fabrics. However, the weave is so tight, I strongly recommend that a very fine needle be used or the stitching can be quite difficult to accomplish and hand quilting is also more difficult. I avoid tone-on-tone prints that read as a solid because my personal bias is against solids. I am much more interested in the texture that a print will create. A tone-on-tone print with good value contrast is valuable to me. I avoid a static print that reads as polka dots. If a little motif is very regularly spaced and the background space is large between motifs, I'll save that fabric for another project. *(1-1)*

The fabrics that you choose will create a theme for your quilt. Clear jewel tones and vibrant pastels will give your quilt a totally different look than the darker, aged looking colors that I used when I made *Prairie Album*. Homespun plaids will give your *Prairie Album* quilt a totally different look than one made from batiks and hand dyes. Quilters are so lucky today. Our quilt shops abound with fabric choices of which our grandmothers could not even dream! You are limited only by your own imagination. So have fun and enjoy stitching your own Prairie Album!

1-1

TOOLS

As with any task, the tools used to accomplish appliqué can make all the difference. I believe it can mean the difference between a really well done quilt and one that is just mediocre. I still appliqué by my philosophy, "the finer the needle, the finer the thread, the finer the stitch."

NEEDLES

My needle of choice is a #11 Straw or Milliner needle. My students really like the Richard Hemming #11 Milliner as the needle has a slightly larger eye and they find that threading the needle can be easier.

Traditionally, appliqué has been done using the Sharp. A Sharp is shorter than the Straw or Milliner and longer than the quilting Between. I find the Sharp too short for me. It pokes a hole in my finger. However, if I use a thimble I can use the Sharp. I will say that personally, I don't like stitching with a thimble, so I prefer the Straw. Whatever needle you like to use, I recommend that you use one with the highest number you can thread. You will have better stitches. *(1-2)*

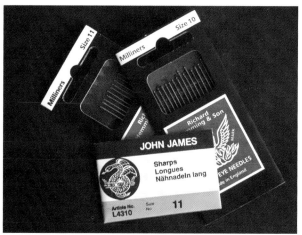

1-2

THREAD

My favorite threads include United Notions' Kinkame Japanese silk, DMC Broder Machine cotton and Mettler Fine Embroidery cotton. *(1-3)* The Kinkame colors blend especially well with Moda fabrics. I use all three threads interchangeably. Color is what drives my choice. My favorite is the silk because it glides so easily through my appliqué fabric, but if I cannot find the color I want I go to the DMC or Mettler. I also like the TIRE silk thread, especially #56, a dark green that blends so very well with many of the greens I use in my work, and #81, a medium green that blends with many more of my favorite greens. When I cannot find the exact color I want, I will use the next best neutral of the same value. A light gray works great for some of the lavender fabrics I've used in other projects. Charcoal gray is a perfect substitute for navy blue. So don't limit yourself to specific colors. Open the thread and lay a strand across your fabric. If in doubt, I go a little darker, never lighter. Remember, you are matching your thread color to the appliqué fabric, not the background fabric.

I find that my stitches are hidden, that is they seem to melt right into the fabric when I use a really fine needle (#11 or #12) and the fine threads described above that match the color of my fabric.

I am able to make my stitches much smaller and closer together when I use the finer needle and fine threads. It is my opinion that quilts should be used and enjoyed, not just stored away to protect them. If your stitches are small and close together, your curved edges will be smoother and the appliqué will be tighter. Your quilt will easily stand up to use.

1-3

SCISSORS

Scissors are every bit as important as the needles and threads you use. I actually have four different sets of scissors that I use for different functions.*(1-4)* When I am cutting the seam allowances around the freezer paper templates, I use a small pair of Fiskars scissors. The blades are very sharp and, if dulling, can be sharpened with a tool that Fiskars offers. They feel good in my hand and after about six years of constant use, they're still sharp!

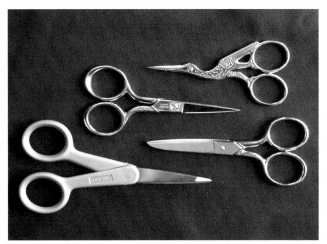

1-4

When I clip the seam allowance on the inside curves or at the inside points, I use 4" embroidery scissors. The tips of these scissors are very sharp and pointed. The very small points allow me to really see what I am doing so that I clip right up to the turn-under line and not through it.

Also, when I clip the seam allowance away from under my sharp points, removing the bulk, I use the 4" embroidery scissors. Again, the tips of the blades are sharp enough and thin enough for me to trim

right next to the last stitch I make, removing the bulk under my points.

When I trim the backing away from behind the appliqué so that I may hand quilt without all the layers of fabric, I use 4" knife-edge embroidery scissors. One blade is the same as the 4" embroidery scissors and the other has a rounded, blunt edge. When I am trimming the background, I make sure that the blunt edge is against the appliqué fabric. *(1-5)* The blunt edge allows the scissors to glide over the fabric instead of inadvertently poking through the fabric. After the first time you have to replace an appliqué piece or create a new one to cover a slice in your quilt, you'll understand why these scissors are so important!

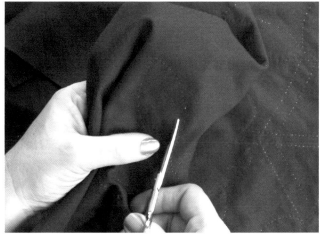

1-5

The fourth scissors I own are the Stork scissors. They really don't do much for me

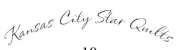

but cut thread. The blades are a little thicker than the 4" embroidery, so they don't do as good a job for me when I'm trimming the seam allowance away for my sharp points. They aren't comfortable enough to cut the seam allowance around the freezer paper templates, as they are pretty small. Any of the aforementioned scissors will certainly cut thread, but the Stork scissors are so cute that I just had to have them!

TEMPLATES

There are a variety of template materials. *(1-6)* Every appliqué artist will have her favorites. They include: template plastic, Con-Tact® paper, mailing label pages, discarded x-ray film, cardboard with aluminum foil, and freezer paper, just to name a few. I think that each project may dictate the template material and method of appliqué and they don't all have to be the same. When I do Celtic style appliqué I use template plastic. I find it easier to remove from the fabric once I have traced it as I don't add a seam allowance to the shapes that will be accented with the Celtic tubes. My very favorite template material for 90% of my work is freezer paper. Freezer paper is relatively inexpensive, easy to trace a pattern through

and can be reused many times. Because I don't wish to do extra steps, I have never used the cardboard and aluminum foil, where you form the fabric around the cardboard template and then hold it in place with the aluminum foil while pressing, but I have tried the Con-Tact® paper and the label page and I still prefer the freezer paper. The freezer paper stays attached to my fabric better than the sticky papers did, and the freezer paper could be reused more, with a better hold. I encourage you to find the materials that work best for you!

1-6

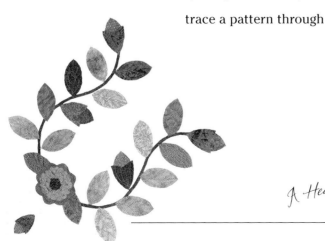

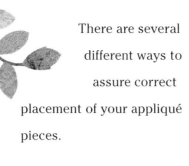

PLACEMENT

There are several different ways to assure correct placement of your appliqué pieces.

You can mark the design on the right side of your background fabric. You'll want to use a light box so that you can easily see the design through the fabric. Mark lightly as these marks must be covered by the appliqué. Once you have finished stitching, you won't want to see the marks. If your background is dark, you might have trouble seeing through it to the pattern even with a light box. Then you have to find a marking pencil that will stay put until you've finished stitching and will wash out if you don't cover it completely with the appliqué.

My favorite method is using an overlay. I like to use a medium-weight clear upholstery vinyl. The light-weight vinyl stretches while the heavy-weight costs a lot more. The medium-weight vinyl does not stretch and has a very reasonable price attached.

With a Sharpie fine point permanent marker (not the ultra fine) I trace the pattern onto the vinyl, making sure that I include the center and side center markings. When it is time to place an appliqué piece,

I line up the center and side center markings on the vinyl with the creases I've made on the background fabric and slip the appliqué piece in between the overlay and the background. The freezer paper template is still on the fabric at this point so it is easy to slip the piece in. *(1-7)*

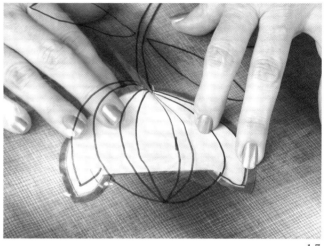

1-7

While teaching the patterns from the *Hearts and Flowers – Hand Appliqué from Start to Finish,* one of my students came up with another great idea! Instead of using the clear upholstery vinyl, she had traced the pattern onto a page protector. (This is an item you can pick up in an office supply store. They are used to protect report pages and come equipped with prepunched holes for placement into a 3-ring binder.) *(1-8)* Now, the value of the page protector as the overlay is two-fold. Not only can it be used as the overlay (the page protector works exactly as the vinyl) but the pocket offers you a place to store your appliqué pieces while they are prepared and waiting for you to apply to the background! You can also store the used freezer paper templates in the pocket for future use if you wish to make the block again and don't wish to literally start from scratch, and, of course, you can place any notes that you may make for future reference. My student even went so far as to have the binding removed from her copy of *Hearts and Flowers – Hand Appliqué from Start to Finish,* and have holes punched into the pages so that she could put the book and her overlays into a 3-ring binder, keeping the whole thing together and secure.

As I see it, the only place that the page protector won't easily work as an overlay is if the pattern is larger than an 8 1/2 x 11" sheet of paper. Speaking of having holes punched into the book, there is something else that I recommend to my students that you may find valuable. I suggest that they take any of their quilting books that they wish to lie flat, to a copy center and have the binding replaced with a coil binding. *(1-9)* The copy centers often have a machine that will slice off the book's binding, punch holes and then apply the new coil binding. The cost, at least in my area, runs anywhere from just under $2 to about $5, depending on the type of coil binding you request. We would love it if the quilting book publishers could do this for us, but the cost of producing our books would be so much more. In the long run, it costs the consumer less to have it done ourselves.

1-8

1-9

PREPARING THE BACKGROUND

Cut a piece of background fabric at least 1 1/2" larger than the finished block. This accounts for 1/2" seam allowance and an inch for distortion while you're working. After the appliqué is completed you will square the block to the correct size.

Before you begin stitching, fold the square of fabric in half and finger press. (Don't iron the crease – it will never come out!) Open the fabric and turn a quarter turn. Fold in half again, aligning the first fold line. Don't worry about the outside edges matching; they will be trimmed away eventually. *(1-10)*

1-10

These fold lines will be lined up with the center and side-center markings on your vinyl overlay when placing your appliqué pieces. I have seen students

fold the square in half and then fold it in half again, without opening out before the second fold. While they think they are being especially careful when they make the crease, the center folds are never exactly perpendicular to each other. I think it is so easy to allow a gap between layers of fabric when folding, much more than with paper. To be accurate, I highly recommend that you make each fold individually so that they are in the correct alignment to each other.

If the print in your background fabric won't let you easily see the finger pressed creases, sew a running stitch for an inch or so at the outside edges and crossing in the center. I use a thread that really contrasts with the fabric so that I can easily see it when I am using my vinyl overlay. My stitches are about 1/8". I backstitch in place to secure it just enough to stay while I finish the block. I want the thread to be easily removed. *(1-11)*

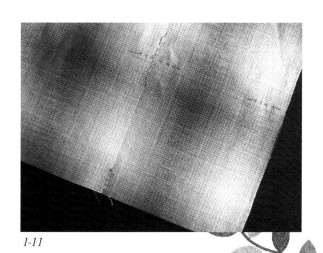

1-11

THE STITCH

I am often asked how it is that my stitches are invisible! In reality, I don't think they are invisible, but I do make every effort to camouflage them so they aren't quite so visible. As I have mentioned before, I begin with the needle (#11 or #12) and thread (fine silk or cotton to match my appliqué fabric) and then I pay close attention to where I place them both.

Now, remember, there are more ways than I use to do everything. I know there are stitchers who work exactly opposite of me. They stitch under the appliqué piece while I stitch over it. That is, their needle is between them and the appliqué. I can only tell you how I do it (and make any sense, anyway). I encourage you to try all the different methods that you can find, and find the one that works the best *for you*!

Right-handed stitchers will be stitching counter clockwise around the appliqué piece. Left-handed stitchers will be stitching clock-wise around the appliqué piece. I hold my needle parallel to the edge of the appliqué as I stitch, and stitch over the edge. That is, the appliqué piece is between my needle and me. I begin with a quilter's knot right behind the turn-under line that I have traced onto the appliqué fabric. Remember, the line is in the seam allowance, so it gets completely turned under. (If the piece I am appliquéing will be overlapped by another piece, I begin stitching where that edge is. If the piece I am appliquéing will not be overlapped by another piece, I begin stitching on a relatively "straight" spot. Never begin at a corner.) So that the tiny knot will not come popping to the surface the first time someone wraps up in my quilt, I take a second stitch in the same place to secure the knot.

With the tip of my needle, I prick the seam allowance and push it under the appliqué piece until the fold includes the turn-under line. *(1-12)* I notice with some of my new appliqué students that they hold the needle perpendicular to the fold as they turn under the

1-12

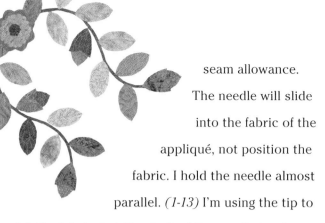

seam allowance. The needle will slide into the fabric of the appliqué, not position the fabric. I hold the needle almost parallel. *(1-13)* I'm using the tip to prick the fabric, but the shaft of the needle is what turns under that seam allowance. The turn-under line is part of the seam allowance and is turned under too. I let my thumbnail oppose the action of the needle so that the appliqué piece does not shift out of placement. (If you bite your nails, OK, but stop biting the thumbnail of your non-dominant hand! It is just as important a tool as your needle and thread.) Once the seam allowance is turned under all the way and the line disappears, the thread should be coming from the edge of the fold that is the turn-under. Place your

needle into the background parallel to where the thread is coming from the fold, but just under the edge of the fold. The tip of the needle should move forward about 1/16th of an inch or less across the wrong side of your background, then up through the seam allowance of the appliqué and out the edge of the fold again.

When I begin stitching with a new appliqué piece or with a new length of thread, I take two stitches in place to secure the knot. The knot is small enough that with any tension placed upon it, the knot could pop right out to the surface of your quilt. Taking two stitches in place will secure the knot and serve to hold it in. Remember, your thread should only be about 18" in length. This cuts down on the number of knots that will plague you.

When you pull the thread to make the stitch, if you have indeed brought the needle out of the fold (not above) and gone into the background just under the edge of the fold (not next to it), the edge of the fold seems to be pulled under a little more and the stitch disappears. If you see the stitch as thread over the top of the background fabric and next to the appliqué, you have gone into the background next

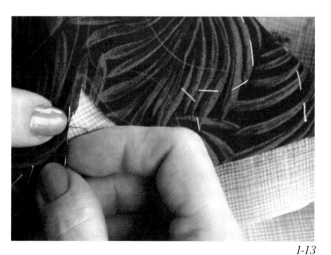

1-13

o the edge of the appliqué, not just under it. If you see the stitch as thread over the edge of the appliqué, you have come out on top of the appliqué, not out the fold, and have literally wrapped the edge of the appliqué with your stitch. If your stitches are hidden but the edge of your appliqué piece looks like tiny scallops, consider loosening your tension – don't pull the thread so tight.

To end stitching, because the thread is getting too short or because I have completed the piece, I don't make a knot. I have a real bias against knots showing on my work, whether it is appliqué, needlepoint, cross-stitch or whatever! Instead, I take my last stitch and then I take another stitch in the direction I just came. I take another last stitch, forward again, and then travel the needle back through the seam allo-wance about an inch. I tug the thread just enough to pull the appliqué a little and snip the thread at the fabric surface. The end then pops back into the interior of the appliqué and disappears. In essence I have made three stitches in place in a figure eight, and that serves to hold the stitching secure.

Just to review, a fine needle with fine thread will make a better stitch. I don't really know why it works this way, and I have students that agree whole-heartedly with this concept. There is a huge difference between working with a #10 needle and a #11. If you are having trouble camouflaging your stitches, I recommend that you change needles.

If you're using a Sharp, try the Straw. If you're using #10, switch to the #11, and don't forget that you must make small stitches close together for your edges to be smooth and your stitches hidden. I know it sounds as if I'm preaching, but I've seen the difference too often not to mention it here!

MORE TECHNIQUES IN NEEDLETURN APPLIQUÉ

RUCHING - HOW DO I RUCHE THEE? LET ME COUNT THE WAYS...

(The following techniques are used in the "Open Bud-Wreath" block and "Rose Spiral" block and the "Swag Border.")

Simply put, ruching is creating texture on a flat surface by creating a series of running stitches and then pulling the thread to gather the fabric, ruffling it. Depending on the shape with which you begin and the placement of the running stitches, the resulting ruching will create a variety of shapes and textures. These shapes and textures can replicate shapes found in nature, such as flowers or bugs, and can add interest, by way of texture, to any appliqué design.

My *Prairie Album* quilt can use two different techniques to accomplish a ruched flower. One method reminds me of a chrysanthemum flower and the other reminds me more of a cabbage rose. The "chrysanthemum" can be accomplished with several techniques and the "cabbage" uses a terrific tool.

I'm going to show you how to make them all and then you can decide which to use in your projects. I have my favorites and expect that you will too.

THE CHRYSANTHEMUM

Any fabric can be used to make the flower, but a multi-colored print will give you much more interest than a solid. The texture of the print coupled with the texture of the flower makes a lovely addition to your project. Then again, I am prejudiced in favor of visual texture! If you like the look of solids, by all means, use them!

Begin by cutting a strip of fabric, selvage to selvage, 2 1/2" wide. With a 1/4" seam allowance, sew the long raw edges right sides together, creating a tube. Turn the tube right side out and press the seam in the center of one side (not along an edge). At this point your tube will measure 1" x about 42". *(2-1)*

Turn in the raw edge on one end and slipstitch to finish. With a 24" length of a <u>sturdy</u> thread, finish

the other end as before, but do not end by cutting the thread. (I use glazed quilting thread to blend with my fabric.) There is nothing worse than getting to the gathering step and breaking the thread in the middle of the process! And, by all means, don't use your good silk thread for this! Leave the thread attached. From this point on, consider the tube as a finished strip with a "right" side and a "wrong" side. You will be working on the "wrong" side (consider the side with the seam as the "wrong" side).

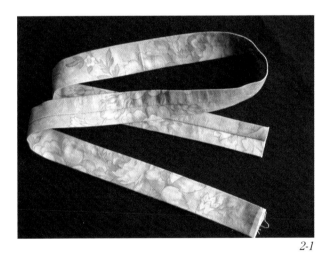

2-1

Beginning at the corner point where the thread is attached, measure in 1 1/2" and mark the spot with a marking pencil *(2-2) (The mark needs to show just enough so that you can see it while you are accomplishing the sewing*

step. I have actually used a permanent marking pen and, when the flower was finished, the marks did not show. A chalk mark may disappear before you are finished with the sewing. I have even used small pins to mark each spot. However, as I stitched I pricked myself a lot and so I prefer the permanent marker to the pins.) Measure the next 1 1/2" and mark again. Continue in this manner, measuring and marking the full length of the tube. Go back to the end where you began and prepare to measure and mark the other edge. From the finished edge with the thread still attached (but not the corner with the thread), measure 3/4" and mark with your marking pencil. This mark should be exactly halfway between the finished edge and the mark you placed when you first began. From this point on, measure 1 1/2" and mark the full length of the tube.

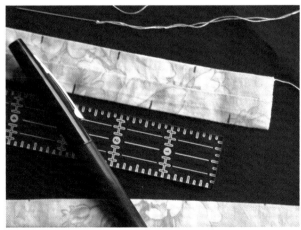

2-2

From the point at which the thread is attached, sew a small running stitch from the corner toward the first mark on the opposite side (the one that measures 3/4" from the end). When you get to the mark, wrap the thread around the edge to the other side and bring the needle through the strip. (If you ended at the mark with the thread on the topside of the tube, bring the needle around to the underside and stitch through to the topside again or vice versa.) Sew the running stitch toward the first mark on the opposite side (the one that measures 1 1/2" from the end) and repeat the step above. It is not important if, when you get to the edge, your thread is on the top or bottom. It is important, however, that you wrap the thread over the edge and begin the running stitch again. Your running stitch will progress along the full length

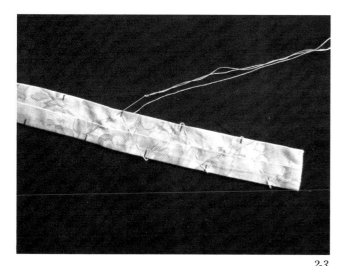

2-3

of the strip in a zigzag fashion from edge to edge.(2-3) As you get to the end of your thread and you approach your last marks, pull the thread to gather

that which you've already stitched and begin sewing your small running stitch until you "run out of thread again." Repeat as needed until you have reached the other finished end. Pull the thread to gather the strip tightly and make a few stitches in place to secure. I take a stitch in place and pull the thread to form a small loop. I put the needle through

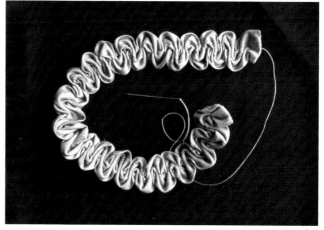

2-4

the loop twice and then pull tight. The resulting knot will hold the stitch so nothing loosens again. DO NOT CUT THE THREAD! You will use the attached thread to secure the flower petals.(2-4) Notice the scallops along the edges of the strip as you pull the thread to gather. This occurs because you wrapped the edge with the thread instead of keeping your stitches all on one side. Now you see why that step was so important!

From the underside of your gathered strip, coil the strip into an ever-widening circle. About every third petal make a stitch by bringing the needle straight up and straight back down through all layers. This little stitch will not show from the front. Continue coiling and stitching until you have used the entire gathered tube and made a circular flower. On the backside, whipstitch the coiled edges to the backside of the flower so the flower is more secure.*(2-5)*

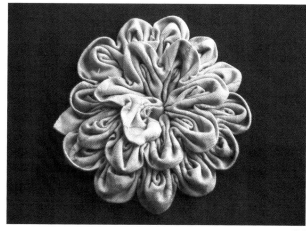

2-6

it is too sturdy and would like a little softer flower. This may be accomplished in two ways.

First, when you are gathering the tube with the running stitches, don't pull your gathers tightly. This will create a softer, looser, larger flower. The gathered strip will be longer if you gather more loosely so you'll have more to coil.

Another way to make a softer flower is to begin with an unfinished tube. Begin with a 2" strip, cut selvage to selvage. Make a 1/2" fold on one long

2-5

Tack the finished flower in place on your block. *(2-6)* You may embellish your flower with beads. These will serve to further secure the flower and add interest.*(2-7)*

The above directions tend to make a very sturdy flower. You may feel that

2-7

raw edge, pressing with your iron to finish the edge, wrong side in. Make a 1/2" fold on the other long raw edge, pressing with your iron to finish the second edge, wrong side in. The raw edges will meet in the center of the back of the strip. *(2-8)* Your strip will be about 1" x about 42".

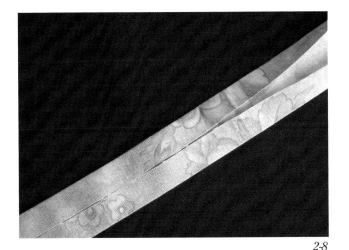

2-8

Finish the ends of the strip as described before, pressing the ends in and whipstitching to finish, leaving a 24" length of thread at one corner. Mark the strip as described above and proceed as directed. When you complete the gathering of the strip, you should notice that it seems softer. There are fewer layers of fabric (no added seam allowance) so it will have less "body" than the first flower. Because there are fewer layers of fabric, you will notice that it is easier to stitch.

You might do some experimenting. I first saw the following done by my friend, Leanne Baraban. Consider cutting strips of two different

fabrics 2 x 21 1/2 " (or 2 1/2" x 21" – depending on the method you prefer) and sew them together to make a strip 42" long. *(2-9)* (Press the seam allowance that combines the two strips open to eliminate bulk.) When you follow the same steps as described above for either method, you will find that you have a two-color flower, which could be very interesting.*(2-10)*

2-9

2-10

THE CABBAGE ROSE

The flower that I like the best has much more flexibility on a quilt. It will add to the drape. The Chrysanthemum, I think, works better for a wall hanging than a quilt, or even for clothing, but remember, that's just my opinion. Please feel free to experiment and decide for yourself!

The Cabbage Rose is accomplished with a "Ruche-Mark Circular Ruching Guide" available from Thimbleworks, designed by Anita Shackelford.

Instead of a strip, this time you begin with a square or circle of fabric. The tool is premarked with little holes spaced perfectly for a variety of sizes. You place the tool over the right side of your fabric and, choosing the size of the flower you wish to make, mark through the holes.*(2-11)*

2-11

When you remove the tool, you will find that the marks are offset, just as your marks on the strip were. Trim your fabric so that you have about 1/2" all the way around past the marks. (The dots on the outer ring are on the fold as you turn under the 1/2".) I like to begin stitching at a dot on the inner circle and stitch to the outer circle of dots, zig-zagging all the way around the circle of fabric. I use a thread to blend with the fabric. (This time you won't have to

2-12

tug so hard on the thread to gather the fabric. While I still don't use my good silk if I can help it, I will use my finer cotton, if I must, to match the color of the thread to the fabric.) Turning under this 1/2" as you stitch, you will sew a running stitch from dot to dot, again, wrapping the edge.*(2-12)* That is, if your thread ends on top when you reach the edge, wrap the thread around to the bottom and bring the needle through to the top and continue stitching to the next dot. Continue in this manner until you are back at the point where you began.

When you've sewn the running stitch all the way around, pull the thread to gather the edge. You can determine the size of the flower by how tightly you gather the circle edge. You will notice that little scallops are formed around the edge and the flat circle takes on the shape of an old-fashioned sleep bonnet or shower cap. I use a ring on the Ruche Mark tool to determine the finished size and check to see if my gathers make the correct circle I'm looking for. The rings don't give me a size for the flower. But then, I never worry about being that detailed. I tend to "eyeball" the circle to the size I like. By setting the gathered circle over one of the rings, I can keep multiple flowers all about the same size. I don't worry too

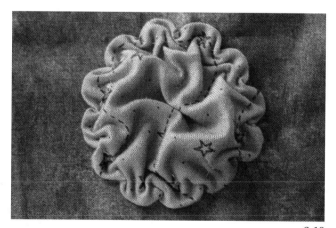

2-13

much about being exact. (You may wish to follow the directions that come with the tool.) When I am satisfied, I tie off just as I described above when gathering

the strip. I appliqué the edges down all the way around to secure. However, I have seen the edge just tacked down, leaving the folded edge to also be dimensional.

Once the edge is secure, I tack the "poof" that is left. I bring my thread up from the back and then go right back down a thread or two away. These tacks create a texture in the center of the flower.*(2-13)* The more tacks you make, the tighter the texture will appear. *(2-14)* The tacks should be taken in the folds so they don't show. Actually, the tacking creates the folds. In addition, the stitches don't show because the thread matches the appliqué fabric. Again, the instructions that come with the tool will give you illustrations to guide you in making your flower.

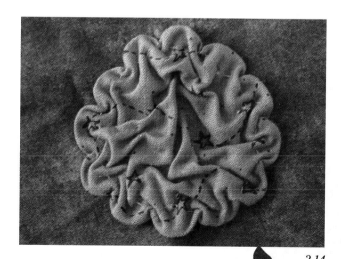

2-14

The tool comes with a chart, as well as the illustrations, that will tell you which marks to use for the size flower you wish to create. It will tell you what size your fabric needs to be and it comes with diagrams showing how the flower is created. Just don't discard the card with all that information!

DIMENSIONAL BUDS
HOW DOES YOUR GARDEN GROW?

(The following techniques are used in the "Rose Spiral" block and "Swag Border" and may be used in "Open Bud-Wreath.")

Dimensional buds add a lot to the texture of your quilt surface and they are fun to make! I'm going to show you a couple of ways to make the buds so you have some choices depending on your project.

A bud often represents a rose and depending on the style of calyx (deep or shallow) you can either make a long bud or a short squat bud. The buds in the *Prairie Album* patterns are the longer version but I'm going to show you how to make both.

PRAIRIE ALBUM BUD

To make these buds, you begin with the calyx. The calyx are the green petals that cradle and hold the

flower petals to the stem. Begin stitching the calyx at the point where I have marked a tiny "x" on the pattern. (If you are left-handed, place the tiny "x" on the other side.) Stitch the calyx to the background, all the way around the calyx to the opposite spot and stop, leaving unstitched the end into which you'll stuff the bud.

2-15

At this point you will need to make your dimensional buds.

Begin with a 4" x 3" rectangle of the fabric that you've chosen for your flower. To make the bud, fold the rectangle in half, wrong sides together, to measure 4" x 1 1/2".*(2-15)* Fold one raw (short) end 1/3 the way diagonally across the center of the rectangle. *(2-16)* Fold the other raw end to overlap but let it be a loose fold so the tip of the bud is a little open. You will have a squared off top to your bud, not a point.*(2-17)*

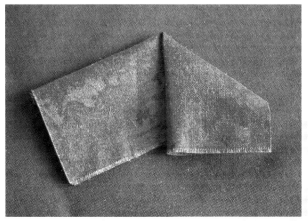

2-16

2-17

into the calyx. Tuck it in far enough so that your gathering stitches won't show at the lowest point

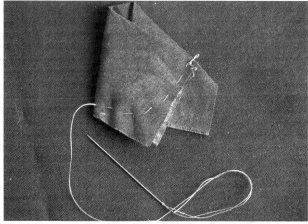

2-18

of the calyx. You will be "stuffing" the calyx where it meets the stem. When you stitch the calyx to the bud, stitch it just to the bud – don't worry about stitching all the way through to the background. Continue stitching the calyx to secure. Tack the back of the bud to the background to secure, but don't catch the front of the bud or you will lose the softness.

With thread the same color as your bud fabric, stitch a small running stitch through all layers across the bottom and pull the thread to gather. (I stitch in a curve toward the bottom. I begin by catching all layers but the middle stitches are only through the overlapping ends. When I get to the end, I am stitching through all layers again.*(2-18)* I do this so that when I stuff the bud into the calyx, the thread is less likely to show above the inner curve of the calyx.) Tie off to secure the gathering.*(2-19)* Tuck the bud

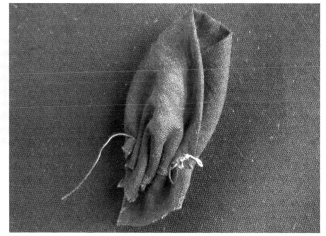

2-19

PUDGY BUD

The smaller, pudgier shaped bud begins with a circle of fabric instead of the rectangle. Do some experimenting to decide just what size you want the bud to be, but start with a 2 1/2" circle. Fold the circle in half, wrong sides together. Fold one end of the half-circle diagonally across 1/3 of the half circle. Fold the other end to overlap the first fold. Fold this edge back on itself no more than 3/16th of an inch to imply a rolled edge of the bud petal. You will have a triangle of fabric with a rounded raw edge.

2-20

With thread the same color as your fabric, sew a running stitch a scant 1/4" from the raw edge through all layers. Pull the thread to gather and tie off to secure. *(2-20)* Tuck the bud into the calyx and stitch as described for making the *Prairie Album* Bud.

Both types of buds are very sweet, but the second style can be made smaller and appear even sweeter. You might do some experimenting. Try sewing two half circles of different fabric together and then fold wrong sides together at the seam. When folded, the bud will have the added dimension of color change. How about using a piece of French ribbon instead of a rectangle of fabric? Some ribbons have a grading in color or value. This would also give the bud an added dimension of color change. If the ribbon has a tiny wire imbedded in the edges of the ribbon, be sure to remove it before making the bud.

CUT-AWAY APPLIQUÉ

(The following technique is used in the "Hot Poker Vine" block and the "Faith" block.)

Sometimes an appliqué piece is narrow enough that you really have no place to put a basting pin except outside the shape itself. Sometimes an appliqué piece covers a larger area or has a very elaborate edge design with lots of twists and turns. Sometimes an appliqué piece combines the two. You might be familiar with Hawaiian and Tahitian style appliqués. I think that the cut-away appliqué technique would be especially beneficial for this type of appliqué. Folding and precutting the shape and then trying to smooth the fabric shape over the background can be cumbersome. Folding and precutting the shape made of paper can be easier. Tracing the paper template onto the fabric and then cutting the seam allowance as you stitch can eliminate a good deal of struggling.

In a nutshell, the freezer paper pattern is ironed onto and traced on the right side of a square of appliqué fabric and then carefully removed. The appliqué fabric is placed over the right side of the background fabric, lining up the center and side-center markings. The two fabrics are basted together with pins or a running stitch. (When you're using a lot of pins, you have a higher probability of the pins falling out and being found by bare feet.) Be sure that the basting is no closer than 1/4" inside the turn-under line. If the area to be appliquéd is very narrow (as in the "Hot Poker Vine" block) you will have to baste outside the appliqué shape. In that case, baste no closer than 1/2" from the turn-under line.*(2-21)* The seam allowance is cut a couple of inches at a time, ahead of where you stitch.(2-22) This is an excellent place to use the 4" knife-edge embroidery scissors so you won't accidentally cut a hole in your background!

2-21

2-22

PIECING THE APPLIQUÉ

(The following technique is used whenever I can piece a unit before appliquéing the whole thing to my background square.)

If you quilt by hand, you're going to want as few layers of fabric to go through with your needle as possible. I know that my stitches will be much smaller and much more consistent if I can reduce the layers of fabric to include one layer for the top, the batting and the backing. Appliqué is at least one layer of fabric stitched to the background (another layer). By cutting away the background from behind the appliqué, you can reduce the layers of fabric to one.

By stitching each appliqué piece to the background, one at a time, and waiting until all of the appliqué is applied to the background before cutting away the background from behind the appliqué, you will have at least one of several problems to overcome. If you cut away the background from behind each appliqué piece, leaving a 1/4" seam allowance, you still have the layers of fabric directly beneath the stitching. If you quilt "in the ditch" around each of the appliqué pieces, you will have more than

the one layer to stitch through. If you try to cut the background fabric away from beneath the stitching by cutting right next to the stitching and working the fabric out from under the stitching, your stitches will be loosened (at least by the thickness of the fabric that is no longer there). You also run the risk of poking the point of your scissors through the wrong fabric and then you have a hole to repair (a piece to replace or add!), which is also a pain!

However, if you can piece the unit (say, a flower) and then appliqué the whole unit to the background you won't have to contend with the stitching between individual pieces. When you cut away the background from behind that flower, you will be left with just the layer of fabric that forms the flower! Your stitches will remain intact and you won't run the risk of making a mistake with your scissors by cutting fabric or thread.

When you are trimming your seam allowances for your individual appliqué pieces, you will need to think ahead and leave more seam allowance in some places. A rule of thumb is to consider that the seam allowance that will be overlapped by another piece is acting as the background to the second appliqué piece. Acting as the background, that seam allowance needs to be large enough to accommodate the pin basting. A 3/16" seam allowance would not be nearly enough to accommodate the pin basting, so I always plan to leave an inch or so.*(2-23)* In other words, piece #1 becomes the background to piece #2 and so on. Once I have stitched the appliqué piece #1 to this background, I trim the seam allowance to 3/16". *(2-24)* Then I stitch #3 to the #1-2 unit, trim the seam allowance and so on. By the time I complete all of the appliqué of the unit, my seam allowances are all trimmed to 3/16". Then I stitch the whole unit to the background, making sure that I begin with the seam allowance of the piece that is farthest away.

When the block is complete, pieced into the quilt top and I'm ready to make the sandwich, I trim the background from behind all the appliqué that will be large enough to quilt in. I don't trim behind stems or tiny leaves or tiny circles or such. I only trim from behind the pieces that I will be quilting in, such as veins in single leaves and around all the petals in a flower.

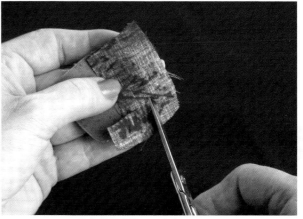

2-24

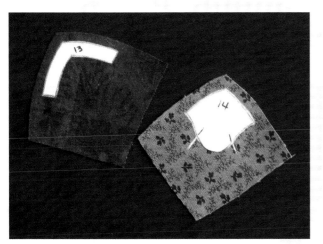

2-23

I tend to wait until the last minute to trim away from behind the appliqué. The background is on the straight of grain, but very often, the appliqué is on the bias. This can weaken the block just enough to misshape it, so I wait as long as I can. (If you use a freezer paper that has a grid printed on it, you could actually position the templates onto your appliqué fabric so the appliqué pieces are appliquéd on the straight of grain. The edges will still be mostly on the bias but the shape will be on grain so that when trimming the background away from behind, the block will not be weakened as much.)

REVERSE APPLIQUÉ

(The following technique is used in "Faith" as well as "Linda's Reel.")

Sometimes appliquéing a shape on top of another shape or the background is difficult because of the shape's properties. If the space is too narrow to fit the seam allowance into, it might be easier to make an opening inside a shape, revealing the fabric of the new shape, so instead of the shape being on top it is actually underneath.*(2-25)* This is called reverse appliqué. In the block called "Faith," I used reverse appliqué to create the vein in the leaf fronds. The seam allowance ended up behind the leaf instead of the vein.

When preparing a freezer paper template for reverse appliqué, the shape may be within another shape (as in the "Faith" block or "Linda's Reel") or it may be that it is the shape itself, such as a feather vine in the border or lettering in the border. A craft knife, used with a rotary cutting mat, makes

cutting a shape out of the center of a freezer paper template easy.

2-25

CIRCLES

(The following techniques are used in the "Tulip Wreath" and "Faith" blocks.)

Circles really add a lot to the dynamics of your appliqué. The smaller the circle, the more impressive it looks. But large circles and small circles are really equal in the ease of making them. The techniques will be slightly different, but they're both pretty easy to make.

Not everyone makes circles the same way. I don't want you to get the idea that there are only one or two ways to make perfect circles. For every "circle maker" there is another set of methods. But I have found, for me, that the following two ways work the best. I give you these directions so that you may find what works best for you.

SMALL CIRCLES

If the circle is rather small, say, anything less than 1/2" in diameter, as you will find in the "Tulip Wreath" block in this book, I don't bother with a freezer paper template. I simply trace the circle directly onto the right side of the appliqué fabric. For one reason or another, I hardly ever use the General's Chalk pencil for this. I want the mark to show and stay put. I don't want to run the risk of the markings rubbing off while I'm still stitching my circle to the background. And because the shape is so small, my thumb covers it as I work. My thumb seems to rub off the markings, unlike when I'm appliquéing any other piece. In fact, I have even been known to use a permanent marking pen with a very sharp point. If I'm using a dark fabric for the circles, I may be forced to use the white marker, but I'd rather not. When using the General's Chalk, however, I sharpen the chalk to a very sharp point so that the line is very narrow.

To draw the circle, I use a circle template, a tool I found in the drafting section of an office supply store. The circle template is made of plastic, often green,

most often translucent for easy placement, and has a variety of circles of many sizes cut out of the plastic. The circles are marked with points indicating the half and quarter, which can come in handy if lining the circles up with straight lines on your fabric. I like the circle template because I find it easier to trace a template from the inside of the shape than the outside (such as a spool of thread or coin). When tracing around the outside of a shape, such as a coin or spool, I always seem to shift the shape or hit my finger and lose the perfect circle. (I hate when that happens!)

After marking the circle onto the right side of the fabric, I trim the seam allowance to no more than 1/8", especially if it is a very small circle. There really can't be any more seam allowance under the circle than there is surface of the circle. Consider your fabric carefully when choosing for the circle. A fabric with a loose weave may not work very well with a 1/8" seam allowance. The tip of the needle may just shred the fabric in the process of turning under the seam allowance. As I stitch, I turn under just enough seam allowance to take one stitch. As I'm working, I've noticed that the work is very influenced by my thumbnail. The shape of my nail often is the most important tool in making the circle! (So, if you bite your nails, you must at least leave the thumbnail alone on your less dominant hand!)

For most of the rest of the stitching that I do, my needle is parallel to the edge of the appliqué piece. But when I turn under the seam allowance for a circle, I prick the seam allowance with the tip of the needle and then as I turn under the seam allowance, I pivot my hand.*(2-26)* This causes the folded edge to curve around the edge of my thumbnail.

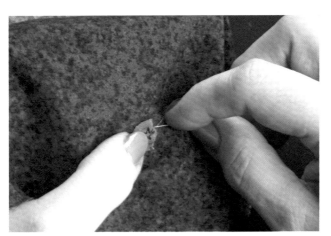

2-26

I am only able to turn under enough to take one or two tiny stitches. After taking those stitches, I prick the seam allowance and pivot again. I continue all the way around the circle until I get back to where I began. Chances are, you are going to have to rearrange the seam allowance for your first stitch so that you won't end up with a flattened side to your circle where you began and ended your stitching. To do this, use the tip of the needle to shift the seam allowance underneath and shape the folded edge. The weave of the fabric lets you mold the fabric as

you wish. Remember, you're in charge! The fabric will do what you want it to! You just have to tell it what you need.

LARGE CIRCLES

A larger circle has a whole new set of tricks to be perfect every time. Again, I don't make a template out of freezer paper. Instead, I make a template using a piece of sandpaper or a heat resistant Mylar template plastic. Let me tell you about sandpaper first, as it might be the easiest to work with if you've never done this before. Begin by tracing the size circle you want on the non-sanded side of the sandpaper with the same circle template you used for the small circles.*(2-27)* I use medium grade sandpaper. I don't want large sand particles on the surface, but I do want the paper to be almost card stock weight. Anything thinner and it won't stand up to the workout I'm about to give it.

Very carefully, cut out the circle. Remember, you are moving the paper, not the scissors while you cut. I use some inexpensive craft scissors but I think the sandpaper helps to sharpen them. I would never use my good scissors though, just in case I'm dreaming! Cut right on the line, inside the line or outside the line. Whatever you choose, however,

2-27

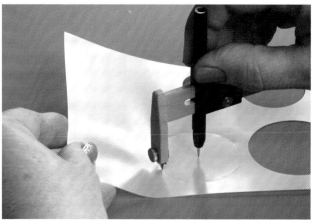

2-28

be consistent all the way around the circle. The better you make your sandpaper template, the better your appliqué circle will be. If after you have cut, you find that the edge of the circle has little pointy spots, use the excess sandpaper to sand the template edge until the circle is perfectly round (or as perfect as you can humanly make it) and smooth. If you like, use an emery board to fine-tune your circle. The stiffness of the board may work to your advantage. I like to use the Mylar template plastic because it allows me to use the Olfa Compass Cutter to cut absolutely perfectly round circles! When using the Olfa Compass Cutter, I turn the Mylar, not the compass, to get a good circle.*(2-28)*

From your fabric cut a square about 1 to 1 1/2" larger than the template. If you are compulsive, you may cut a circle out of the fabric that is about an inch or so larger than your template. I don't usually waste

my time, however. The square works just fine. Place the template, sanded side next to the wrong side of your fabric. You will be holding the template while you accomplish the next step. The sand keeps the template from slipping around while you work. (You may also use Mylar template plastic for your template; however, you will want to trace the template onto the wrong side of the fabric and set the template aside while you accomplish the next step. The plastic is slippery and won't stay put like the sandpaper.)

Thread your needle with a sturdy thread such as hand quilting thread. I use my #10 Straw needle for this instead of my #11. The eye is large enough to accept the thread and the needle won't bend as easily. I don't care what color thread I use. I just want it to be very strong. It won't be seen. Make a good, sturdy knot on the end you cut. If making a quilter's knot, wrap the thread three or four times instead of

A Heartland Album

two. Make a series of running stitches about 3/16 of an inch away from the template; remember you're working on the wrong side of the fabric and holding the sandpaper in place with your thumb. I make long stitches (about 3/16 of an inch) and short stitches (about 1/8 of an inch).*(2-29)*

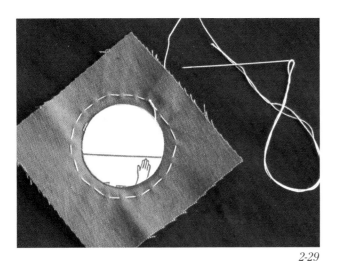

2-29

The stitch that I make on the wrong side of the fabric (I can see the needle) is the long stitch, while the stitch on the right side of the fabric (I can't see the needle) is the short stitch. When I have gone all around the circle, I bring the needle to the right side of the fabric. Then I pull the thread, gathering the fabric around the template. (If you are using a Mylar template plastic form, be sure to place it back onto the wrong side of the fabric before pulling the thread to gather the fabric.) Use your needle to distribute the gathers around the template so that you eliminate

any pleats that will cause the edge to have any points. The smoother you make the edge, the more perfect your circle will be. Pull the thread tightly and then make a knot to hold the gathers in place. I make a loop and pass the needle through it twice to make a secure knot. Double check to see that you have no pleats on the edge.

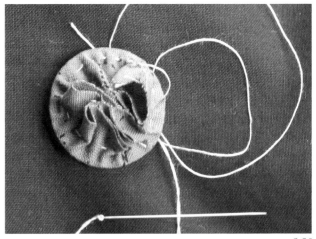

2-30

If you have a great deal of fabric gathered on the back, lop off the portion that is sticking up at this point. Don't "trim" anything. Just lop off what amounts to the corners of the square with which you began. Don't worry how it looks. It has nothing to do with the final results. *(2-30)*

With a hot steam iron, press the form on one side and then the other. I use a block of clean wood that has been sanded smooth, and left unfinished, to absorb the moisture and heat after I press.*(2-31)* I learned this when I used to make tailored clothing items like my husband's suits or my winter coats. The wood absorbs the heat and the steam and sets the crease. In other words, hold the iron down on the template, and immediately upon lifting the iron, hit it with the wood. After a few seconds, remove the wood, turn over the template, press with the iron and hit it again with the wood. I make a bunch of circles at once if I have need of many circles on a block. That means I need to make a template for each of the circles. I let the covered templates cool and dry thoroughly before I appliqué them to my background.

2-31

Before stitching, cut the back away around your stitching with the 4" embroidery scissors, leaving about a 3/16-inch seam allowance. The very sharp points of the blades come in very handy for this. You then peel the template out and you are ready to pin the circle to your background and stitch. I place my pins perpendicular to the edge when I pin baste circles and I only use three pins. If you do end up with any minor "points" around the edge of your circle, you can eliminate them. As you stitch you can use your needle to pull the seam allowance under just a bit more to compensate.

FIXING A CIRCLE

No matter how careful we are when stitching a curve, there are times that we just cannot get that curve to be perfectly smooth. We end up with little "points" along the edge. Making our stitches too long usually causes these little points. I recommend that you stitch your circle to the background with as small a stitch as you can possibly make and close together. But, if you do end up with little sharp spots around your circle there is a remedy!

Remember, you are in charge when you appliqué, not the fabric! Sometimes you have to get a little tough (tough love?), but your quilt will thank you for it. Once you have stitched a curve that did not curve quite right, you can go back in and repair the curve without unstitching anything.

When I have a curve to fix, be it on the edge of a circle or any other curve, I go into the seam allowance between the background and the fold of the appliqué with the tip of my needle. I prick the seam allowance and tug it until the offending curve is corrected. Before letting go, I use my thumbnail to press a crease into the new edge of the appliqué. No one can ever tell that it has been repaired! Unless that missed stitch is just really long, long enough to get my fingernail under, I don't restitch. I just press with my thumbnail.

If the offending curve is a tiny circle, I may have to take more drastic measures to get it to be round. I thread my needle, make a quilter's knot and bury the knot between the appliquéd circle and the background. I bring the needle out just to the side of the offending spot and then bring it back into the appliqué just on the other side, around a stitch, and bring the needle out again on the opposite side just next to another offending spot. When I tug the thread and press with my thumbnail, the first offending spot gets pulled in toward the center, causing the edge to appear to be more round. I repeat this process, going back and forth across the circle, until I am satisfied with my circle. I pull the thread through the seam allowance to the opposite side of the circle and clip the thread tail just at the fabric surface so as to hide the tail within the appliqué. And, voila! My circles are perfect!

FREEHAND BIAS STEMS

I have already told you about using the 1/4" Bias Tape Maker to make stems for your blocks. Beginning on Page 46, I'm going to tell you how to make stems using the Celtic tubes made from bias strips and Celtic bars, but sometimes you have a need for a bias stem and you don't really need very much, certainly not enough to warrant the trouble of making the bias tape or the Celtic tube.

You can easily make bias stems free hand!

First, determine the length of your stem. You can set a ruler next to the pattern and "guesstimate" the length, *(2-32)* or you can lay a piece of string next to the pattern and then measure the string. Add an inch to the length for good measure. Determine the width of the stem. If it is 1/4" or narrower, I cut my strip about 1" wide.

center, one side of the fold is wider than the other. On the wider side of the fold, lay a ruler along the fold so that the edge of the ruler is the same distance from

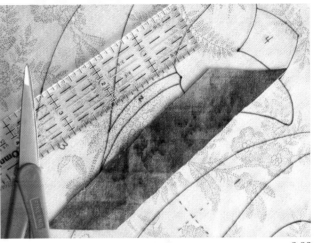

2-33

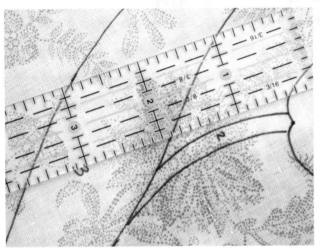

2-32

Next, cut a bias strip of fabric. I just cut with scissors and I don't worry about how accurate I am.*(2-33)* Even if the strip is not cut on the true bias, it will work. I cut my bias strip about an inch or so wide by the length I need plus an inch long.

Right (or left) of center, I finger press a crease the length of the strip.*(2-34)* Because I have folded off

the fold as the stem should be wide. In other words, if my stem will be 1/4" wide, I lay the ruler along the fold so that the 1/4" mark is on the fold and the edge of the ruler is 1/4" away. With a marking pencil that will show on my fabric (dark on light fabric and light on dark fabric), I make a line along the edge of the ruler.*(2-35)* Now I'm ready to stitch.

If the stem pattern has a curve to it, lay the folded edge on the background so that it runs along the inside curve. Make sure that the stem extends 1/4" past the ends of the stem so that it will be overlapped by the next appliqué piece. Sometimes I make a mark on my background, lightly, that is just the inside curve of the stem. Most of the time I use the placement overlay and place the fabric, again, so that the folded edge is along the inside curve. Pin-baste in the direction that you will be stitching.

2-34

2-35

Stitch the folded edge to the background as you usually do. It is important, however, that you stitch that inside curve first. When the stitching is complete, lay the folded fabric back, exposing the seam allowance underneath. With your 4" knife-edge embroidery scissors (blunt tip against the background so you have no accidents) trim the excess seam allowance to 3/16" or less if the stem is less than 1/4" wide.*(2-36)*

Trim the opposite seam allowance 3/16" wide or less if the stem is less than 1/4" wide. Now, with your needle, turn the seam allowance under, including the line that you marked, and stitch the outside curve.*(2-37)*

That's all there is to it. It's a free-hand stem that is very simple to make. I use this technique if the stem is fairly short and if I don't have any extra bias tape made. I also use this technique if my stem is narrower than 1/4". If my stem is just 1/8" wide, I trim the seam allowance on the inside curve very close to my stitching. If I have made my stitches short and close together, I should not have to worry that my seam will come loose or that my seam allowance will ravel. The seam allowance on the outside curve is cut 1/8" wide. Using this method, very narrow seams are really quite easy.

2-36

2-37

BUTTONHOLE STITCH APPLIQUÉ

Another method of adding a little texture to your appliqué is to stitch the appliqué to the background using the buttonhole stitch. This stitch overlays the edge and adds interest and an outline at the same time. Depending on how close together you place your stitches, you could have a light and lacy edge or a heavy and solid looking edge. Personally, I prefer the light and lacy look.

I strive for my stitches to be as far away from one another as they are long. In other words, if my stitches are 1/8" long, there will be 1/8" between stitches as well. The size of the appliqué pieces will dictate the size of the stitch. A very large shape may support stitches that are 1/4" long with 1/4" intervals. A small piece, as found in the blocks for the *Prairie Album* quilt, will require smaller stitches. Whatever the length of your stitch, you should strive for even stitches.

When I begin stitching, I knot my thread with a small Quilter's Knot and then I bring the threaded needle up from the wrong side of the background just next to the edge of the appliqué shape. If you take a stitch over just one thread of the background you will secure that knot. I pierce the appliqué shape with the needle 1/8" to the right of where I began and 1/8"

from the edge. I bring the needle up again from the wrong side of the background just next to the edge of the appliqué shape and 1/8" to the right of where I began, catching the loop of thread behind the needle.(*2-38*) This creates a straight 1/8" stitch perpendicular to the edge of the appliqué and a straight 1/8" parallel to the edge of the appliqué. I do all of this from the right side of the fabric. That is, I do not poke stitch at all. The needle does all of the traveling from the right side. My needling hand does not go to the wrong side of the fabric.

As I get to an outside point of the shape, my stitches will still be 1/8" apart and 1/8" long, but the stitch that goes into the appliqué shape may well be going into the same hole for a total of three stitches. (*2-39*)

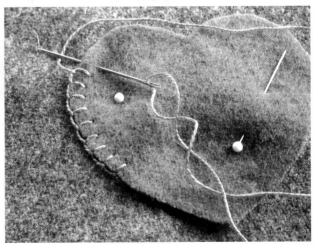

2-38

As I get to an inside corner of the shape, my stitches will still be 1/8" long but they may not be 1/8" apart. The stitch that goes into the background may well be going into the same hole for a total of three stitches.*(2-40)*

2-39

To end, I poke the needle down through the same hole in the background, catching the loop, and then tie off on the background.*(2-41)* Since I have a thing against knots, I tend to travel the thread through five or six of the stitches on the backside and turn and travel back the way I just came, wrapping my thread around the last stitch before turning, and clip the thread.

This is 2/3 of the figure 8 and I think this secures the thread just fine. There are no rules regarding the color of your thread for the buttonhole stitch.

2-40

Matching the thread to the appliqué fabric will make the stitches just a little less noticeable. A contrasting color may add another element of interest. Using black or navy around all of the appliqué shapes will give another element of interest yet. I suggest you experiment a little to find the look that suits you and your project.

2-41

TRAPUNTO

Another method of adding dimension to your appliqué is to add a "fill" to the design. Stuffing shapes with batting or string is called Trapunto. Webster's Dictionary defines trapunto as "a decorative quilted design in high relief worked through at least two layers of cloth by outlining the design in running stitch and padding it from the underside." There are several great books out there on the whole subject of Trapunto. I'm only going to go into it a little – just to tell you what I do. While it is possible to do this process on your sewing machine, I prefer to do it by hand.

Begin with your fabric choice. A light colored solid is the best choice. A dark solid doesn't let the design show up very well. A print won't let the Trapunto show at all. If you have an aversion to solids, as I do, you might choose a print that is a tone on tone and where there is so little contrast between the values of the color that one has to look very closely to see that the fabric indeed has a print.*(2-42)*

Next choose your pattern. When choosing your pattern, you'll want to choose a design with distinct shapes. I find that a simple design is the most effec-

2-42

tive and provides the most drama.

With a water-soluble marking pen, trace your pattern onto the right side of your fabric. Place a piece of batting, larger than the size of your design, on the wrong side of your fabric. I like to choose a batting that has some loft to it. If I want a really puffy look to my Trapunto, I will choose a medium-high loft polyester batting. But mostly I use the batting that is 80% cotton and 20% polyester. This batting provides enough loft for my purposes. I use a few pins to hold the two pieces together while I stitch.

Next you'll need a thread that contrasts with your background. I don't use my silk thread for this. Any piecing thread will do as long as the color is not the same as the quilting thread you will be using. You want to be able to easily see the thread for removal later without mistaking it for the quilting. With a small running stitch, baste the fabric to the batting just inside the drawn line, about 1/16."(2-43) When two shapes are right next to each other, stitch each one separately, just inside the line about 1/16." I do all of the work from the right side of the fabric. That is, my knots are all on the top. This way I can clip them later and easily pull the threads as I finish.

When I have finished basting the batting to the fabric I cut away the excess batting. With my 4" knife-edge scissors (see the scissor discussion on page 10), I clip right next to the basting stitches around each of the shapes. When two shapes are right next to each other, there will be a channel between the two when I have completed the clipping.(2-44)

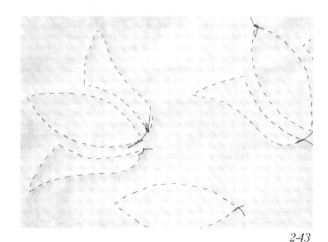

2-43

When you are completely finished removing the

excess you will be left with just the fabric and batting shapes.

Now you're ready to sandwich your top and quilt. Use the same methods you use when hand quilting a finished top. I choose a thinner batting for the sandwich. I think it makes my Trapunto work show up a little better. (When making a pillow using Trapunto for added interest, the backing I use is just muslin. No sense in using a good fabric since it will be hidden inside the pillow.) Your Trapunto will show up better when the quilting you do around the Trapunto is close together. So heavy quilting in the background is preferred. Please note, however, that for your quilt to lie flat or hang straight, the entire surface will have to be quilted with a consistent density. I think the biggest mistake we quilters make is to get tired of the quilt

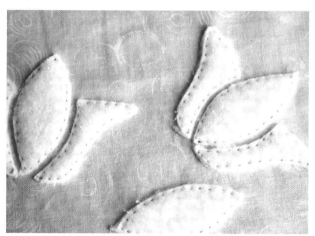

2-44

by the time we reach our borders and skimp on the quilting in the borders. You might have to force yourself to keep up the quilting in the borders, but you'll be rewarded if you do!

Once you have finished all of the quilting around the Trapunto, you may remove the basting stitches. Just clip the knots on either end of the basting and pull the basting thread. The quilting that outlines the shapes and the quilting in the background will hold the batting "stuffing" in place.

Your final step is to wash out the water-soluble marking pen. Just misting the fabric with water will make the marks disappear visually; however, the chemicals will remain in the fabric. It is possible that the marks will reappear years from completion, and the marks will be dark and permanent.

Submerge the quilt in cool water and soak for 20 minutes. Then rinse thoroughly with cool water to wash out the chemicals. Never use warm or hot water, as it will only serve to set the marks, not remove them.

CELTIC APPLIQUÉ

(This technique was used to create Whispers in the gallery of quilts.)

Celtic Appliqué is a design element harking back to ancient symbols and designs often seen in an ancient religion. The designs appear to be wonderfully intricate knots made from a continuous rope with no beginning and no end. What I have done with *Whispers* technically is not Celtic. There are no intricate knots (unless you consider the border design as a series of knots), and the designs are really quite simple. In reality, I have used some elements of the Celtic knot idea to add an outline to my appliqué. By manipulating a "rope" around the shapes I have implied a continuous knot that accents the appliqué and adds interest.

Begin by choosing simple designs. If there are too many sharp curves, you may find that adding the accents is less than an enjoyable endeavor. Appliqué is supposed to be fun and relaxing!

Before I played with the Celtic appliqué process, there were two absolutes for me. The first was that I only wanted to use freezer paper for my templates. Freezer paper was the easiest for me, is reusable and fairly inexpensive.

The second absolute was that I only wanted to make my bias tape with a Clover Bias Tape Maker. Even if I wanted to work with 1/8" bias, I used the 1/4" Bias

Tape Maker to begin. I had seen the bias tubes made with the Celtic bars and didn't like the *idea* of the bulk caused by so many layers of fabric. In addition, making the bias tape was so much easier than the bias tubes because it eliminated the step that required a sewing machine. However, in the pressing of the fabric, as it goes through the Bias Tape Maker, the bias strip of fabric does get stretched some. You simply cannot help it! The stretching that occurs means that the bias tape isn't as flexible as the bias made with the Celtic bars. Up until I used the bias as an accent around the appliqué, the limited flexibility did not affect my work. I recommend that the bias you use for the Celtic appliqué most definitely be made using the Celtic bars. You will appreciate the flexibility! The bulk that I was so concerned about is non-existent!

Although I had never actually used them, over the years I had collected bias-making bars, both made of plastic and metal. *(2-45)* I started with plastic because they cost relatively little. However, I wasn't as happy with them because I saw that they were rather thick, too thick to create a good crease in the pressing step. I worried about the metal bars, though, because I was concerned about burning my fingers in the pressing step. Eventually, I tried the metal because they were thinner than the plastic. I thought that if I were very careful, maybe I wouldn't burn myself too badly and the crease would be sharper. I was right about the sharper crease and I didn't burn myself. Actually, I never have burned myself using the metal bars. With the heat, the plastic bars warped and the metal ones didn't as much. So, I recommend that you get the metal bias bars for your work. They truly are the better product for my purposes.

The first time I tried the Celtic appliqué process, I used my familiar freezer paper as the template. With this process I don't add a seam allowance and so I found it rather difficult to remove the freezer paper without distorting my fabric and fraying the edges. So, for this process I recommend template plastic.

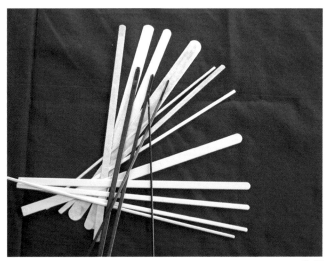

2-45

The rest of the tools that I use for Celtic appliqué are the same that I use for needleturn appliqué. Same needles, same thread, same scissors, same placement overlay.

To begin, trace your pattern onto the clear upholstery vinyl for your placement overlay. Be sure to add the center and side center markings. Then trace your pattern onto template plastic just as you do for needleturn appliqué. (That is, where possible, trace the design as a whole, and cut apart instead of tracing each individual shape separately.)*(2-46)* I use a permanent marker instead of a pencil so that the markings won't rub off onto my fabric. Include the stitching sequence numbers. Cut the plastic templates with paper scissors.

Place your template onto the right side of the appliqué fabric. I recommend that you use your sandpaper board under the fabric. Without the freezer paper, your fabric is even more unstable and is, therefore, more difficult to mark. Trace the template onto the right side of your appliqué fabric. I have been known to use a permanent pen if the fabric is light enough in color for the pen marks to be seen.

Cut out the appliqué shapes with fabric scissors. The pieces that will be outlined with the Celtic bias do not

2-46

get seam allowance added when cutting. If you will be mixing needleturn with Celtic, be sure to add the seam allowance to those pieces. If another will overlap one piece, add 3/16" seam allowance just where it is to be overlapped. Do not add seam allowance to the edges that will be covered by the accent Celtic bias and will not be overlapped by another piece. *(2-47)*

Your stitching sequence is just as with needleturn appliqué. Begin stitching in the order given on the pattern. I still made my stems with the bias tape maker. I still liked eliminating the step that calls for the sewing machine whenever possible. You may wish to use the Celtic bias bars for consistency. There are no rules!

The appliqué shapes are then basted to the background. I use very

small running stitches and I stitch no further from the edge of the shape than 1/16". *(2-48)* These stitches will be covered by the bias accents, so I don't worry about the color of my thread. I don't use my silk thread in this step due to cost, but I do use the fine cotton. I don't want to add bulk by using the thicker thread. This may all be in my head regarding the bulk, but just to be safe, I use the finer thread. Where one

2-48

just make one line of basting stitches.*(2-48)*

2-47

piece overlaps another, I tuck the seam allowance that I included under the second piece. The first time I did this process, I gave myself no seam allowance. I butted the two pieces together and then had two sets of running basting stitches to cover with the bias. I really didn't like the results. So, learn from my mistake and overlap the two pieces and

Once all the appliqué pieces are basted in place, you are ready for the Celtic bias. I used the 1/8" bias bar. The directions that came with my set of bars says that for 1/8" bias I am to begin with a 3/4" bias strip. It would not hurt you to make that bias strip wider. It may, in fact, make it a little easier for you to work with. The length of the strip needs to be as long as it takes to go around the appliqué shape with an inch or so extra. I found that cutting a bias strip from 1/2 yard pieces of my fabric was enough for the lengths I was working with in *Whispers*. However, anytime the bias passes under itself, a break is allowed to occur, so you can get away with shorter lengths if need be. Once it is stitched, it will still look like one long continuous strip.

Begin by determining where 1/8" lies from the needle on your sewing machine.*(2-49)* You will probably have some landmark on the throat plate or the

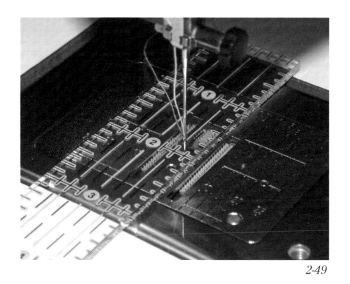

2-49

Fold your bias strip so the wrong side is together and begin stitching the length of the strip so that the stitching is a consistent 1/8" from the fold.*(2-51)* Do not expect to stitch with the 1/8" bias bar within the fold. It won't work. The next step is to insert the 1/8" bias bar into the tube, taking care not to stretch the fabric. The bar will not fill the full length of the tube depending

presser foot that you will be able to follow. If not, you may wish to mark the 1/8" spot with some masking tape. The important thing to remember is that the fabric needs to be in contact with the feed dogs. I found that if I aligned the folded edge of the bias strip 1/8" to the right of my needle, my fabric moved along nicely. When I reversed it, I had all sorts of problems trying to sew a straight and consistent seam. You may have to do some experimenting to determine if you need to move your needle off of center or even orient the fold to the left of the needle. Your feed dogs may be positioned differently than mine. I also discovered that using a solid foot was easier than an "open toed" foot.*(2-50)* The open toe allowed the fabric to ride up into that crevice between the "toes" and I lost my accuracy. (I had a student try to use a zipper foot, but her stitching line was all over the place. When she switched to a larger foot, she became very consistent.)

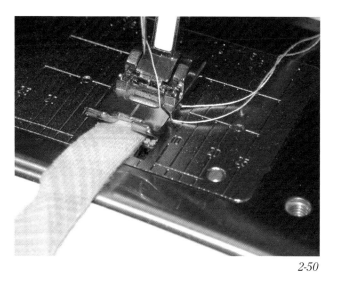

2-50

on the length of your bias strip. Twist the seam allowance so that it is oriented to the flat side of the bar.*(2-52)* I twist just until the stitching is just over the edge, making sure that none of the thread will show along the edge. With a hot steam iron, I press the seam allowance over the flat side of the bar toward the center.*(2-53)* The raw edge of the seam allowance will probably extend past the fold on the side opposite

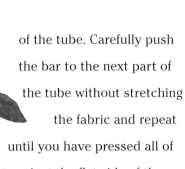

of the tube. Carefully push the bar to the next part of the tube without stretching the fabric and repeat until you have pressed all of the seam allowance flat against the flat side of the bar. Remove the bar.

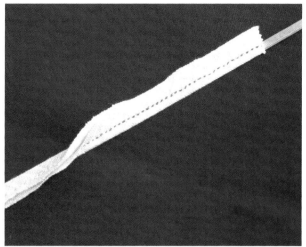

2-52

2-51

will be secured between the top of the Celtic tube and your background by your hand stitching. It will never show and it won't ravel and come apart, especially if your stitches are small and close together.

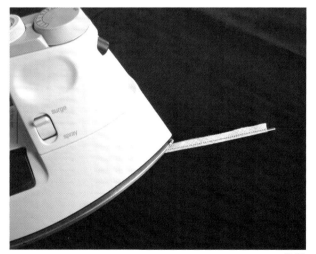

2-53

With your very sharp embroidery scissors (I use the 4" embroidery scissors), trim the seam allowance right next to the stitching.(2-54) The smaller scissors allow you to get closer to the stitching. I leave no more than a thread or two's width. (You'll probably be trimming about 3/16" of fabric away.) Don't worry about raveling. The stitching and very narrow seam allowance

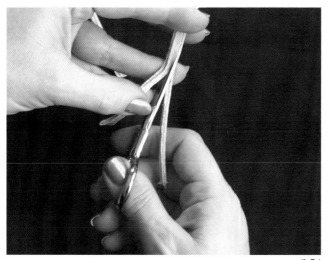

2-54

another length to overlap the raw ends of the first. I encourage you to look closely at the blocks in *Whispers* to study what I did. I tried to use a variety of blocks so that you could see several ways to use the Celtic accents. *(2-55-2-59)*

When you stitch the Celtic accent to your appliqué there are only a couple of things to remember: 1) Stitch the inside curve first and, 2) a finished Celtic tube will overlap raw ends. Study your design and determine your route, remembering that you will be stitching the inside curve first. Sometimes you can use one continuous tube to go all around the shape. Sometimes you will use one length for pieces towards the back and

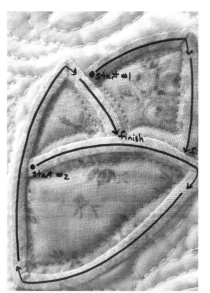

2-55

2-56

Begin stitching the Celtic tube to cover the basting. I don't bother with pins. I use my thumbnail to hold the tube in place and I "sculpt" as I go. *(2-60)* I also begin stitching with the bulkiest edge first. This way I am sure that the seam allowance is tucked in securely if in my pressing I missed the mark when I twisted the stitching to the flat side of the bar.

2-57

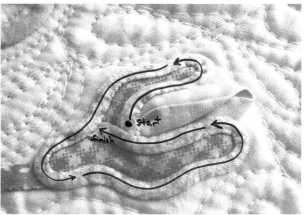

2-59

This creates a miter for me. I take another stitch to secure that inside point and continue stitching. When I get all the way around, I tuck the raw edge under the Celtic tube I've already stitched into place. Then I turn around and stitch around the outside curve. I begin and end in the same spot. Each Celtic accent is stitched twice, on both sides of the tube.

At a point, miter the "corner." I make a stitch at what I determine to be the inside point of the miter. With my needle I grab the edge about 1/8" ahead of the stitch and fold and tuck in behind the tube I've already stitched.*(2-61)*

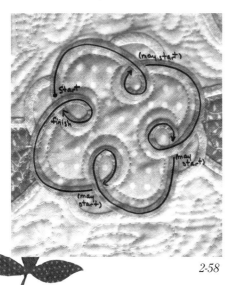

2-58

2-60

If you are counting, each appliqué shape is actually stitched three times: basting, Celtic tube inside curve and Celtic tube outside curve.

The Celtic accent can be used for almost any design. If you notice, however, in my quilt *Whispers* I did have to make some adjustments. The "Hot Poker Vine" block used a combination of the Celtic and needleturn. The stems are much too thin to accent with the Celtic tube so I only went around the leaves. The ends of the Celtic tube are tucked under the stems.

If the design you wish to accent with this method includes very small pieces, you might consider using a combination of Celtic accents (for the larger pieces) and needleturn (for the smaller).

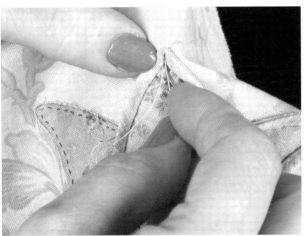

2-61

Prairie Album
by Kathy Delaney, Overland Park, Kan.
Quilted by Jeanne Zyck
93"x 93"

PRAIRIE ALBUM

Fabric Requirements

Block Background:

>2 1/2 yards of 44" wide fabric **OR**
>
>1 2/3 yards of 59" wide fabric

Appliqué Border Background:

>2 2/3 yards of 44" wide fabric
>
>(add 2/3 yards for binding) **OR**
>
>2 2/3 yards of 59" wide fabric
>
>(you'll have enough for binding)

Block Appliqué fabrics – You will need a variety of fabrics for the appliqué. I bought 1/3-1/2 yard pieces when I was planning the quilt so that I would have pieces wide enough for bias tapes. I'm always willing to have too much; I can always use it again later, but I sure don't want to run out in the middle of the project! You may find that fat quarters will be enough for most colors. They certainly are wide enough for the bias tapes. But you may find that you won't have yardage enough of two or three fabrics for the whole quilt (those that tend to be your favorites that you will use more often). I suggest that you get 1/2 yard cuts of your favorite two greens and favorite red. To that end, you will need:

>For leaves and stems – 8 or 9 greens, ranging from light to dark
>
>For flowers, flower centers, motif – 5 or 6 golds (I chose a muted or "old" gold, ranging from medium bright to dark.)
>
>For flowers, buds, motif – 5 or 6 reds, ranging from bright to dark (One of the reds will be repeated in the appliqué border.)
>
>For stems, leaves, flower centers – 2 or 3 blues, ranging from medium to dark (One of the blues will be repeated in the sashing and appliqué border.)

Sashing:

>1 1/2 yard of a "background" – that is, a fabric similar to, but not the same as your block background fabric – a fabric that coordinates with the block background
>
>1 7/8 yard of a "contrast" – that is, a fabric that is darker or lighter than the sashing "background" – a fabric that reads as a solid and stands out – subtlety is not what you want here (I used one of my appliqué blues.)

Additional yardage for appliqué border:

>2 1/2 yards of your contrast fabric that you're using in the sashing for the swag
>
>1 1/4 yards of one of your reds for the swag – determine which of your reds you like the best and want to live with the most
>
>1 yard of one of your darker greens for the vine that repeats around the border
>
>1 yard of one of your golds for the ruched flowers that repeat around the border

(One fabric will provide an elegant look. A variety of fabrics will cause a busier look – which you may like! **Hint** – don't use up any of your scraps from this project in another quilt until you are finished making this quilt top as you'll need them for the border appliqué design – especially the reds for buds – and you won't want to run out!)

You will also need:

>1/4" Bias Tape Maker
>
>1/2" Bias Tape Maker

THE APPLIQUÉ BLOCKS

From your block background fabric, cut (12) 19" x 19" blocks. You will trim these to 18 1/2" x 18 1/2" after you have completed the appliqué and before you sew them together with the sashing. Prepare each of the background squares as described on page 14.

Block 1
"Open Bud-Wreath"

Block #1 – "Open Bud - Wreath"

Trace the pattern onto a piece of clear upholstery vinyl. See "Placement" on page 12. I traced the first half of the pattern onto the vinyl and then <u>flipped</u> the vinyl to trace the first half again. The transparency of the vinyl made it simple! (Note that the numbering on the shapes represents the stitching sequence. The "r" refers to the fact that the leaf shapes are also used in the same order on the "reverse," or left, side of the open wreath.

From one of the 1/2 yard green pieces, and using a rotary cutter, mat and ruler, cut (3) 1/2" wide bias strips (across the full width of the fabric). With your Bias Tape Maker, make (3) strips of bias tape. (I store my bias tape wrapped gently around an empty bathroom tissue core. This maintains the crease in the tape and eliminates wrinkles.)

With a mechanical pencil, trace and number the leaves onto freezer paper, drawing on the side that is not shiny. (Hint: Each of the leaves is the same shape and size. You might wish to make one template from template plastic and use that one shape to trace all of your freezer paper templates. It could save you some time.) Cut the freezer paper templates out, adding nothing for seam allowance. With the shiny side against the right side of the leaf fabrics, press with a dry iron, set on the wool setting, for a few seconds. Placing the template so the majority of edges are on the bias of the fabric ensures an easier needleturn appliqué process. With the appropriate marking pencil, and placing the sandpaper board under the fabric, trace around the freezer paper. Cut around the paper adding a 3/16" seam allowance. Leave the freezer paper attached until ready to stitch. The freezer paper makes it easier to position the appliqué piece under the placement overlay. Repeat with #12, #12r, #14 and #14r.

#11, #11r, #13 and #13r are buds. The process is the same; you'll just be using your red fabrics.

#15 is an appliquéd flower that serves as a base for a ruched flower. Use the method of your choice as described in "Ruching" beginning on page 19 for your ruched flower.

center

3/c

4/c

5/c

6/c

1/c

2/c

1/c

2/c

7/c

15

T

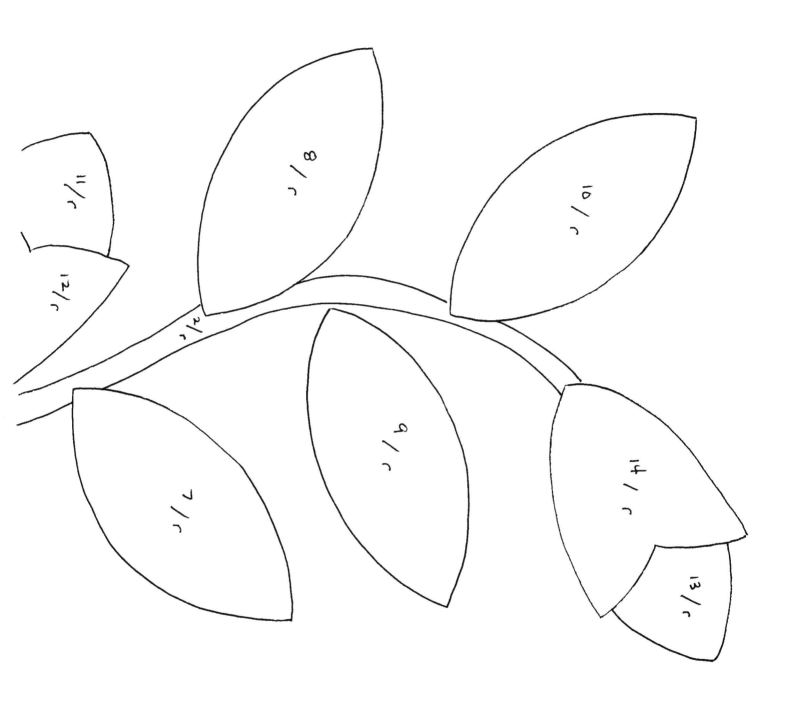

Block 2
"Rose Spiral"

Trace the pattern onto a piece of clear upholstery vinyl. See "Placement" on page 12. You will need to trace the block pattern two times (pattern is shown as one half of the block design), if you want a placement overlay showing the whole pattern. Or, just make the half overlay and <u>rotate</u> the placement overlay around the center for placement of your appliqué on the other half of the block, stitching one half at a time. Rotating the overlay is important to note: If you flip the overlay as you did with Block #1, you will not get a "spiral" but a "crab." *(3-1)*

From one of the 1/2 yard green pieces, and using a rotary cutter with a new or newly sharpened blade, mat and ruler, cut (3) 1/2" wide bias strips (across the full width of the fabric). With your Bias Tape Maker, make (3) strips of bias tape. *(3-2)*

Trace the pattern pieces onto the paper side of freezer paper, numbering the pieces as they appear in the pattern. The numbers indicate the stitching sequence. Stitch all the #1 (bias stem) pieces first, the #2 (bias stem) pieces next, #3s then #4s and so on. The buds are made at the same time as you stitch the #7s and #8s. Refer to "Dimensional Buds" on page 26. A ruched flower, to cover the raw ends of the center is done last. Refer to "How do I Ruche Thee…" beginning on page 19.

(You may want to keep the templates for the calyxes and use them again in your border.)

3-1

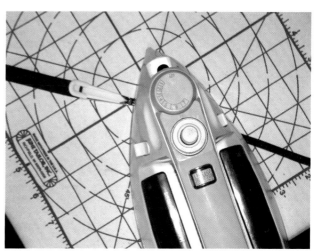

3-2

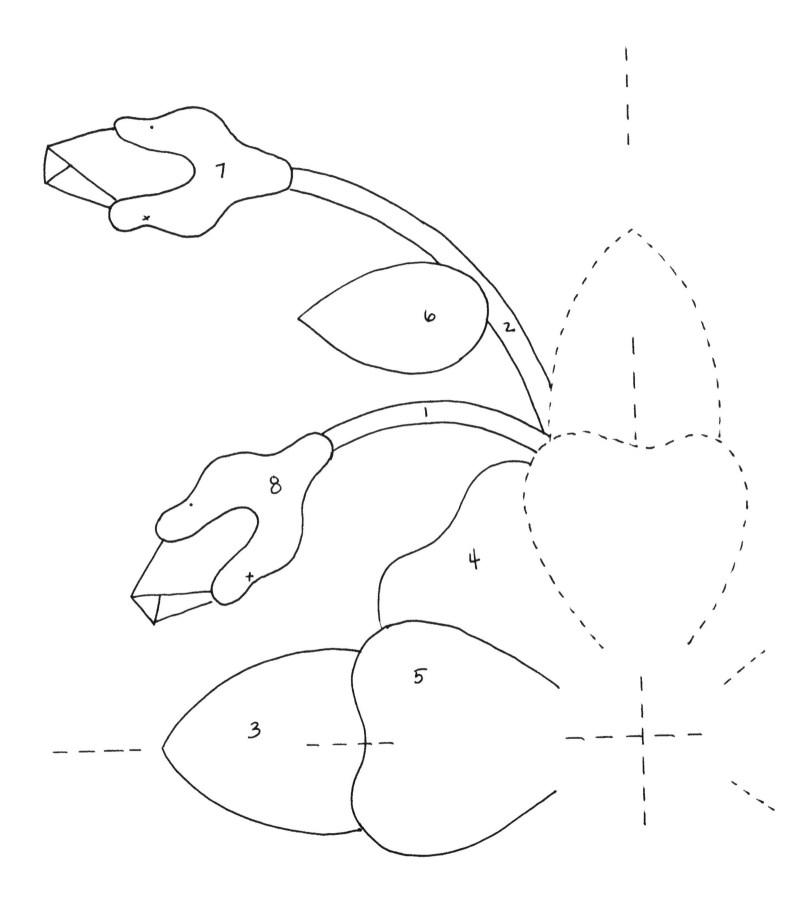

7

6

2

1

8

4

5

3

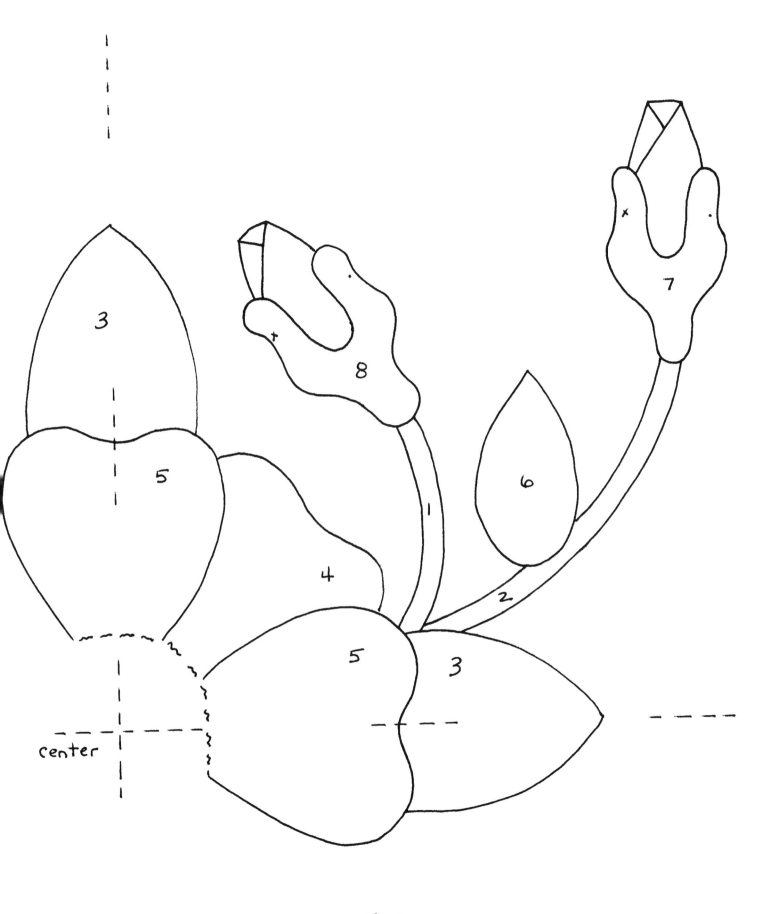

center

Block 3
"Hot Poker Vine"

Block #3 - "Hot Poker Vine"

Trace the pattern onto a piece of clear upholstery vinyl. See "Placement" on page 12. I recommend that you trace the block pattern four times around the center to create a full pattern (pattern is shown as one quarter of the block design). You will have an easier time with your template placement if your placement overlay shows the whole pattern. Rotate the pattern around the center to create the overlay as well as creating template #1.

To make your freezer paper template, begin by marking the side center and center markings on the non-shiny side of your freezer paper so that you can properly line up the pattern quarter. Then fill in the template shape, rotating the pattern around the center. With your paper scissors, cut out the shape for template #1 and iron it onto the right side of your green appliqué fabric using the "wool" setting on a dry iron. Another way would be to cut four squares of freezer paper, making sure that one corner is perfectly square on each of the four pieces of paper. Trace the pattern onto the non-shiny side of one of the squares. Stack the four pieces of freezer paper with the shiny side down on all, aligning the center with the squared corners. Staple the center of leaves to secure the folded paper. Cut through all four layers at once.*(3-3)*

Iron onto the right side of your fabric, matching the center corners. Trace around the template with the appropriate marking pencil but **do not** trim your seam allowance yet. The stems of the vine are quite narrow, so be careful when handling the template or it will tear. (A freezer paper "bandage" ironed onto the non-shiny side of the pattern at the tear should repair it.)

3-3

Remove the template from your appliqué fabric by running a long pin or needle between the freezer paper and the fabric to release the hold.*(3-4)* This keeps the fabric

from stretching as it would if you just pulled the freezer paper from the fabric.

Center the appliqué fabric over the background using your overlay as a guide. (Or, mark the green fabric showing the center and side-center markings and align these marks with the creases on your background.) Baste the two fabrics together with a running stitch on the outside of the appliqué shape, no closer than 1/2" from the turn-under line. If you have matched the center and side-center markings you will notice that the design is slightly twisted off center.

Begin in one of the corners (they will be overlapped by the red leaves, #2, #3 and #4) and cut a 1/8" seam allowance. Only cut about 2 inches. Begin turning under the seam allowance with the tip of your needle and stitch about 1 1/2".*(3-5)* Trim more seam allowance about 2" ahead. When you get to the leaves, you will have to use your small appliqué pins to keep the leaves from shifting. As you cut more and more of the excess away, you can discard the excess. It will only get in your way. Clip the basting thread and remove it from the excess to be discarded. The rest of the basting will stay in without knotting it.

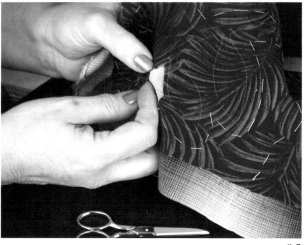

3-5

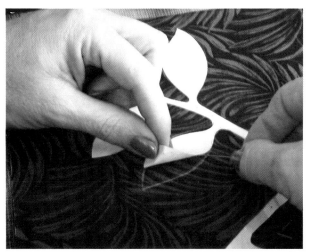

3-4

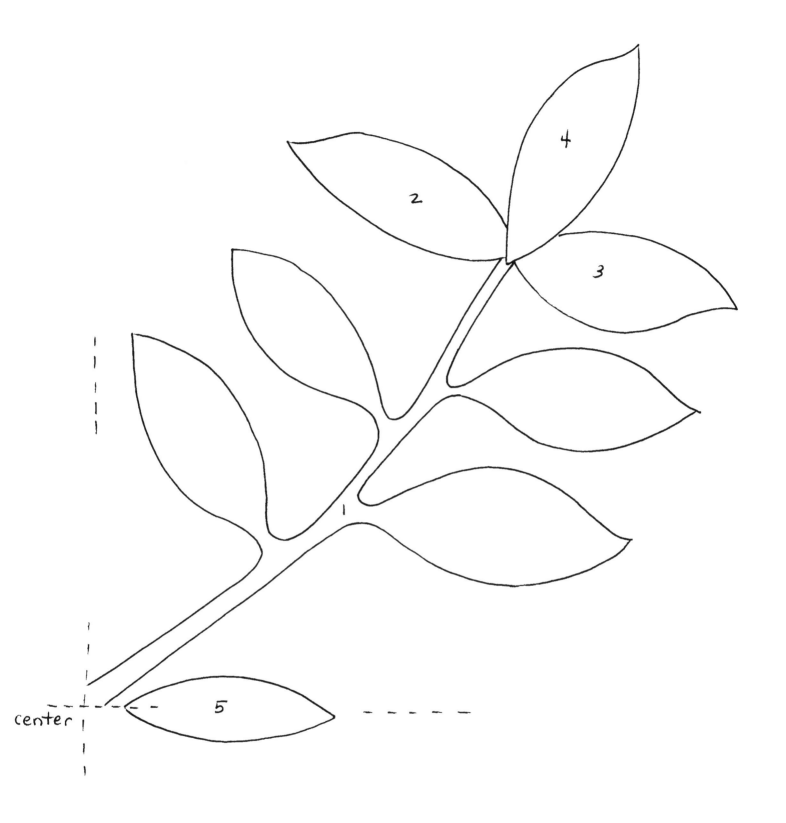

4

2

3

1

5

center

Block 4
"Love Apples"

Block #4 – "Love Apples"

Trace the pattern onto your placement vinyl. See "Placement" on page 12. This time the pattern is shown as a full half of the pattern so that you can see that the center stems twist around each other. Use the two parts of the pattern to create half the overlay and then <u>rotate</u> to create the other half.

On the non-shiny side of the freezer paper, trace the templates for the apples, leaves and hearts. Since layering makes the Love Apples, you are going to have to trace each of the shapes separately. This is a departure from my usual method of making freezer paper templates. Be sure to extend the lines where #1 intersects #3 so you can line up the pieces more easily when you get ready to stitch. Don't forget to transfer these marks to the seam allowances. (Note: #3 is a solid circle shape, not 3 separate pieces.)*(3-6)* Remember making

valentines in grade school? I still cut my heart shapes by drawing only half and then folding the paper to cut both halves at once.*(3-7)*

You may wish to piece the appliqué for the four Love Apples before appliquéing to the background. Just be **sure** that you leave an opening at the base of the apple shape into which you will insert the stem. I also left the center of #1 as a solid piece of fabric until after #3 was appliquéd to it. It gave me something to hold and something to pin #3 to. After stitching #3, trim the seam allowance, eliminating the layer of fabric behind #3.

The stems are again made with the 1/4" Bias Tape Maker and stored on an empty tissue core.

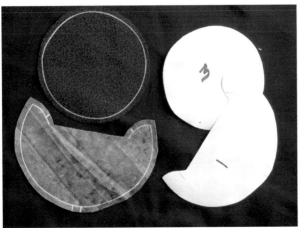

3-6

3-7

center

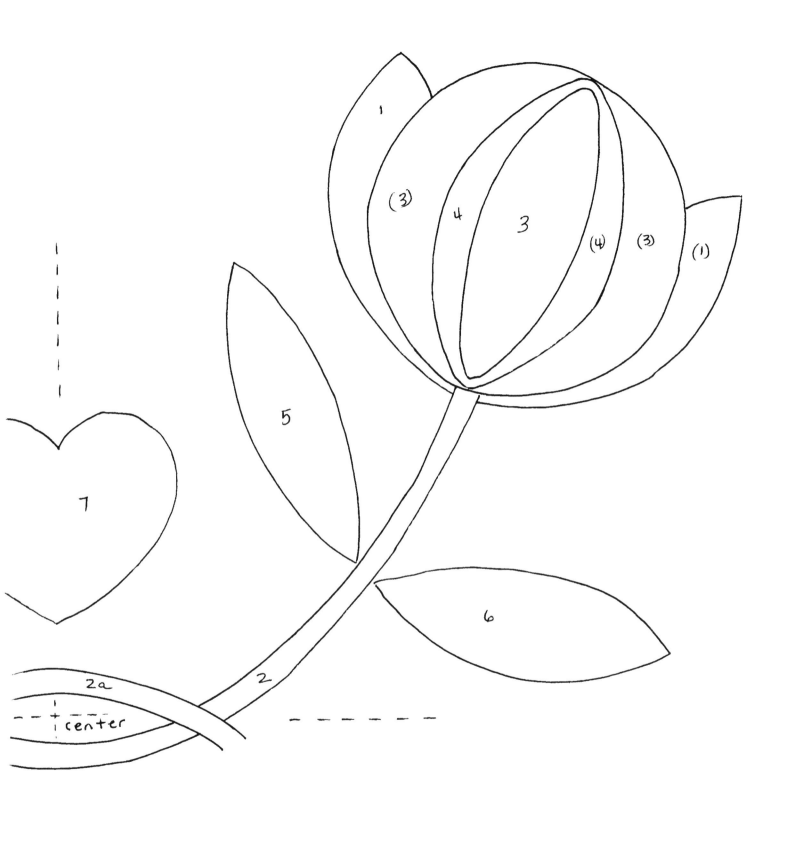

1

(3)

4

3

(4)

(3)

(1)

5

7

6

2a

center

2

Block 5
"Tulip Wreath"

Block #5 – "Tulip Wreath"

Trace the pattern onto your placement vinyl. See "Placement" on page 12. The pattern is shown one half of the full pattern. You may wish to trace the pattern two times to make your placement overlay. By rotating the overlay you will form the full wreath, just as you did with the second block, "Spiral Rose."

You may wish to piece the appliqué tulips before stitching them to the background. I try to piece everything before stitching the appliqué to the background. Besides letting me cut the background away from behind, there is less for me to have to hold while I stitch. Instead of making three separate templates for each flower, you may trace #4 and #5 as one piece. I simply extended a line to connect the two outside petals. *(3-8)* Once #6 is stitched to the petals #4/5, you will want to trim the excess away from behind #6. *(3-9)*

The stems are made with the 1/4" Bias Tape Maker. Do you have any left from a previous block? I would suggest that you take some time to make several lengths of bias tape from each of your greens. Storing them on an empty bathroom tissue core keeps them from wrinkling and from relaxing the crease. When you are ready to stitch, the tape will already be made.

The curve of stem #1 may give you a little trouble since the inside curve is so deep. To eliminate extra bulk on that inside edge that will look like the fabric has been gathered, stretch just the outside edge. By pulling the outside edge between your fingers you will stretch just the outside edge of the curve. The bias tape will curve and lie flat for you.

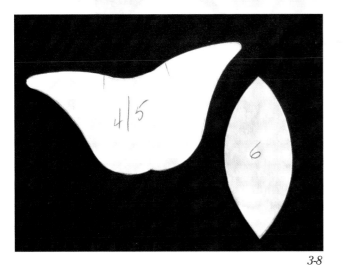

3-8

3-9

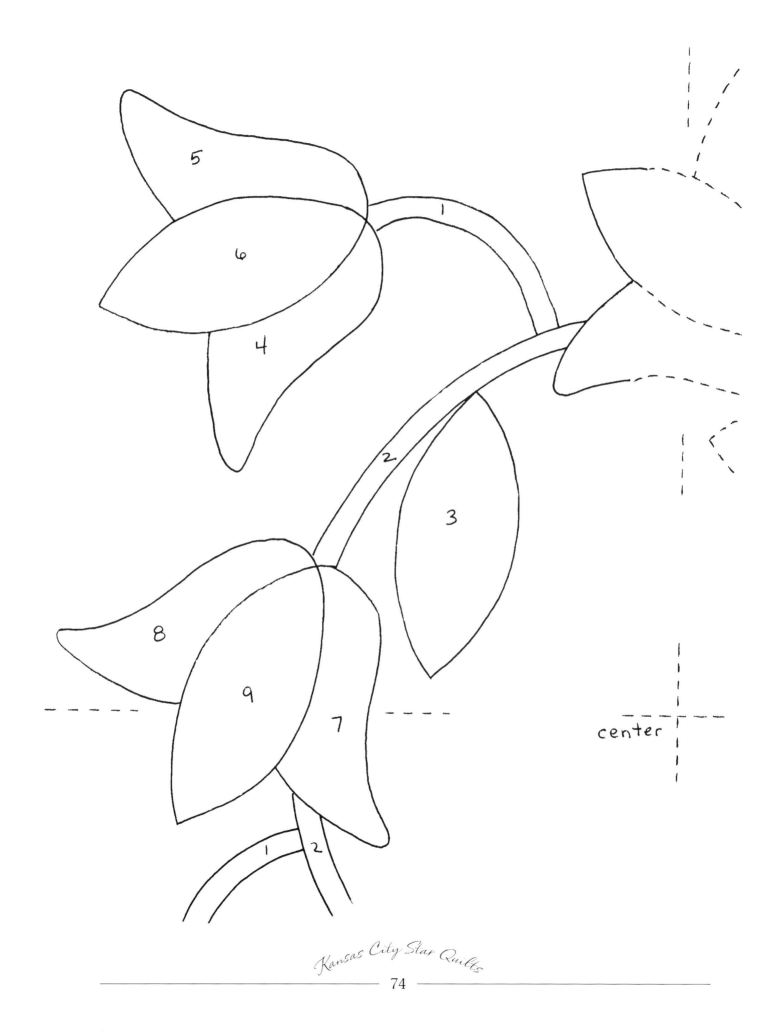

center

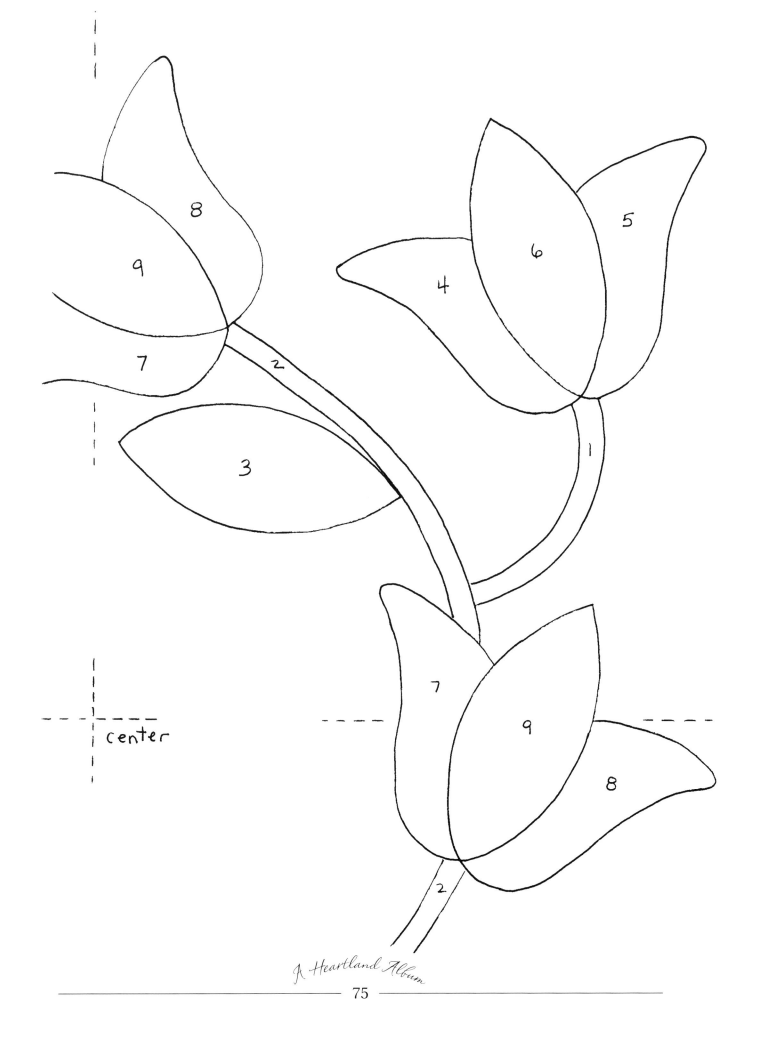

center

A Heartland Album

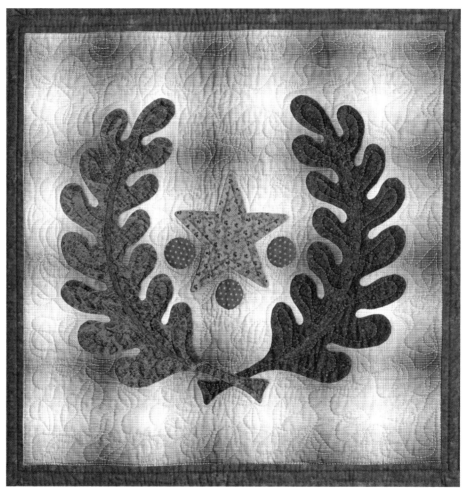

Block 6
"Faith"

Block #6 - "Faith"

Trace the pattern onto your placement vinyl. See "Placement" on page 12. The pattern is shown as half of the full design. This time, <u>flip</u> the pattern to create the full pattern. (I traced the one side of the pattern onto my vinyl and then tuned the vinyl over and traced the first side again next to the first tracing. Since the vinyl is transparent it was simple!)

When I made my freezer paper templates for the leaf fronds, I traced a leaf once. Then I placed another piece of freezer paper, shiny sides together, under the tracing. I stapled the two pieces together so they wouldn't shift while I cut and then cut the shape out, cutting two leaves at the same time, in mirror image.*(3-10)* Before I removed the staples I carefully cut the veins (#1a) out of the center of the leaf fronds with a craft knife and discarded them. You will not be using these as templates. When you iron the template onto the right side of your fabric and then trace around the template with a marker, you will also be tracing in the opening as well.
(3-11)

3-10

The fabric that will represent the vein in the leaf will need to be about 5" x 10 1/2" and it will be placed, right side to wrong side, behind the leaf fabric. To make sure the rectangle will fit completely behind the vein, I stuck a pin straight into the leaf fabric at the very ends of the vein and then another one about half way down the vein on the right side, the outermost edge of the outside curve.

When I lined up the vein fabric under the leaf fabric, I used the pins to make sure I had the two fabrics lined up properly and had extra vein fabric all around the vein.*(3-12)* About 1/2" from the traced lines representing the vein of the leaf fabric, I pin-basted the two fabrics together.

With very sharp scissors (I use my 4" knife-edge embroidery scissors with the blunt tip against the vein fabric), cut the leaf fabric as I have indicated with the dotted line on the pattern. This is the seam allowance that is turned under to reveal the vein.

I wait to cut this line until the two fabrics are layered. I have found

3-11

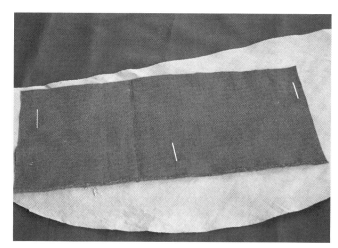

3-12

that lining up the two fabrics is much more difficult when the vein opening is cut first. I end up exposing more of the vein fabric than I intended. This then distorts my block. Remember to clip inside curves (in this case that's the outside edge of the veins) and with your needle, turn under the seam allowance and stitch the leaf fabric to the vein fabric. As you stitch, you will be revealing the vein fabric.(3-13) When you have stitched the leaf fabric all around the opening revealing the vein fabric, turn over the piece and

trim the seam allowance of the vein fabric to 3/16", discarding the excess vein fabric or using it in another appliqué project. Now you are ready to appliqué the leaves to your background.

Once the veins are stitched into the leaf fronds, you can stitch the leaf fronds to the background square. Because you have, in essence, pieced the appliqué, you will have no trouble trimming the background from behind the appliquéd leaves so that quilting "in the ditch" around the veins will be easy. In my humble opinion, quilting around the veins adds

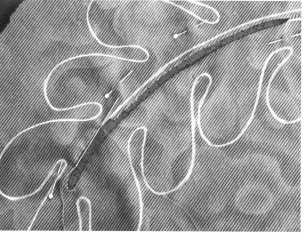

3-13

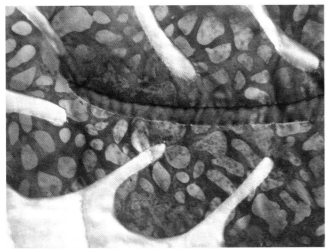

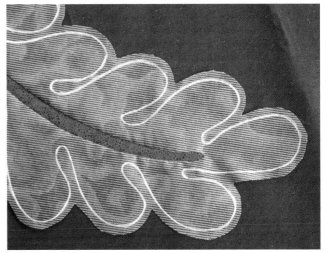

3-14

dimension and interest to the block.*(3-14)*

You will need a template for the star but not for the circles. Refer to "Large Circles" beginning on page 34 for details that will lead to perfect circles.

You may find that the cut-away appliqué technique will work best for you when you appliqué the leaves on the "Faith" block. Actually you have a choice. You may decide to cut the seam allowance around the outside of the leaves and then just clip those seam allowances at the deep inside curves when you get to them.*(3-15)* That's how I did the block. You will only need to make three small clips into each of the deep curves to form the smooth edge.*(3-16)* Remember not to clip through the turn-under line. Use the shaft of your needle to swipe the seam allowance under and secure the edge fold with your thumbnail as you stitch.

3-15

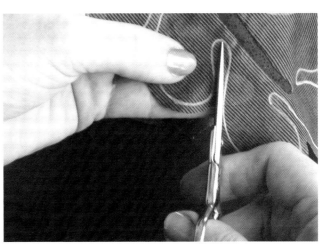

3-16

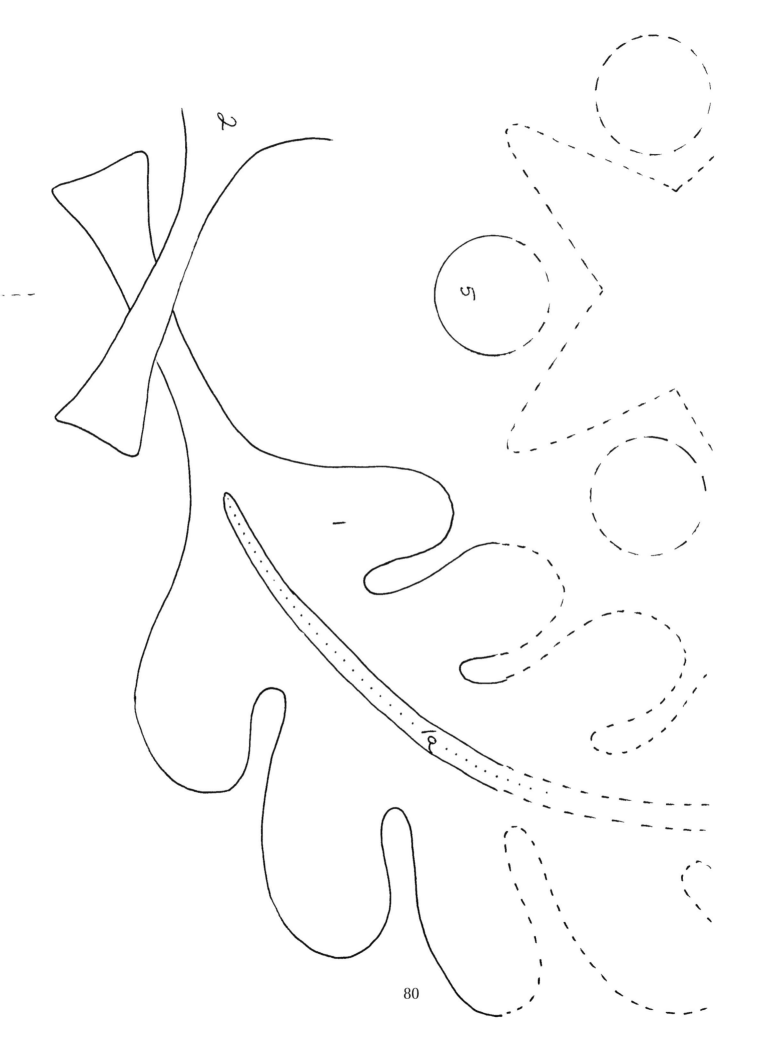

80

4

3

center

5

6

1a

1

81

Block 7
"Prairie Flower"

Trace the pattern onto your placement vinyl. See "Placement" on page 12. The pattern is shown one half of the full pattern. You may wish to trace the pattern two times to make your placement overlay. By <u>rotating</u> it around the center you will form the full wreath.

When I made this block, I pieced each of the appliqué units before stitching them to the background. Tiny circles #10 were stitched freehand, onto the flower #9. That is, I didn't make a form. I used my circle template and traced the circles directly onto the right side of the fabric and I used a permanent pen with a very fine point.(3-17) I didn't want the ink to

run and I wanted a very fine turn-under line. See "Small Circles" beginning on page 33 for full details. You may need to use a light marker to show your fabric.

For circle #11, however, I used the template forms. See "Large Circles" beginning on page 34 for full instructions. I traced the template for #9 onto the right side of the appliqué fabric but I didn't trim the seam allowance until after all the circles were complete.This way I didn't run the risk of causing my seam allowances to ravel from handling the piece while I stitched.*(3-18)*

3-17

3-18

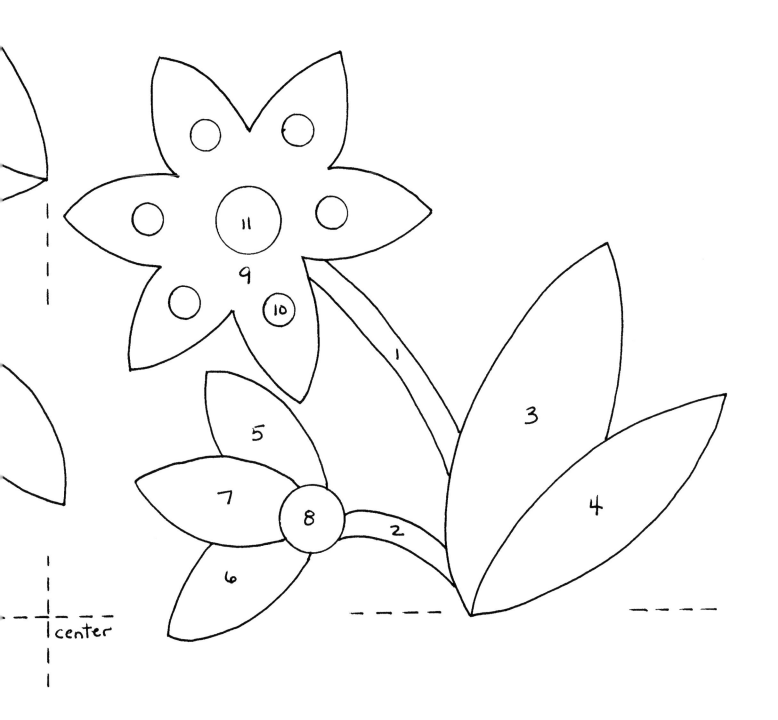

center

Block 8
"Welcome"

Block #8 – "Welcome"

Trace the pattern onto your placement vinyl. See "Placement" on page 12. The pattern is shown one half of the full pattern. You may wish to trace the pattern two times to make your placement overlay. By <u>rotating</u> it around the center you will form the full design.

Undoubtedly, you have noticed that the deep inner points of the leaves don't allow much of a seam allowance. Depending on how you draw your pattern, you can determine how much seam allowance with which you will have to work. I know that this looks just about impossible. But believe me, you can do this! There really is enough to turn under – not much, but enough! By taking small stitches close together, you'll be able to secure such a small amount of seam allowance. Take your time. You will really use the point of your needle to turn under only enough seam allowance to take one stitch. Your thumbnail on your non-dominant hand will be very important here. Just don't forget to breathe! As you get to the deepest part of the inside point you will use your needle to swipe away from you, turning under the seam

3-19

allowance.(3-19) There really will be nothing for your needle tip to grab. So you will need to continue the turned under fold with the shaft of your needle. If you just find yourself frustrated to the point that you're not having any fun, go ahead and take a deeper seam allowance. The fun is the most important part of appliqué! Your leaves will appear a little narrower than the pattern shows, but so what? It's your quilt! Who's going to know? The Quilt Police don't know where you live and I'm not going to tell them! Before you give up, though, give it a try as drawn. You might surprise yourself!

The outside points may be a little trickier as well. The process is exactly the same as you have been doing but you will want to take smaller stitches and to trim your seam allowance to really eliminate the bulk. There just won't be room for excess fabric. (See *Hearts and Flowers* for a review of points.)

4

3

5

6

2

1

Block 9
"Linda's Reel"

Congratulations! You've made it this far and you're ready to use all of what you've learned on this block, your final exam. There is nothing in this block that you haven't already done on one of the other blocks in this quilt.

Trace the pattern onto your placement vinyl. See "Placement" on page 12. The pattern is shown one half of the full pattern. You may wish to trace the pattern twice to make your placement overlay. By <u>rotating</u> it around the center you will form the full design. Like "Open Bud-Wreath" and "Faith," the two halves are mirror images. If you wish to, you may flip the vinyl to trace the second half.

Just by looking at the pattern though, you might have trouble knowing exactly what is intended, so let me give you a list of techniques to use with the individual pattern pieces. You will appliqué all of the pieces, in the order of the numbering, finishing with the reel in the center. Once you have stitched all of the leaves and stems, you will be ready to add the flowers.

Piece the appliqué #14 onto #13. Trim the excess away from behind #14. Reverse appliqué #15 onto

#15a. (Notice that #15a does not need a template since it is revealed in the reverse appliqué process. When making your templates out of freezer paper, use a craft knife to cut out the space labeled #15a.) Turn it over and trim 3/16" seam allowances around the stitching on the #15a.*(3-20)* Piece the appliqué #15 unit onto the #13/14 unit. Trim away the excess from behind #14. You will stitch #16 last. Again, trim away the excess from behind #16. The whole unit then gets appliquéd to your background.

3-20

#11 and #12 are ruched flower centers. I used the circular RucheMark tool from Thimbleworks. See the complete description beginning on page 24.

THE SASHING

The following directions show the cutting instructions for 40 inches of usable fabric — selvage to selvage. The instructions for the 57 inches usable fabric will appear in [ ]. If both fabrics are 57" wide, follow the directions in [ ]. If one of the other or both are 40", follow directions for the 40". Unless otherwise noted, all "cutting" is done with a rotary cutter and rotary cutting ruler; the strips are cut across the fabric from selvage to selvage.

SASHING STRIPS:

From the background fabric, cut (12) 2 1/2" wide strips [(8) 2 1/2" wide strips]. From the contrasting fabric, cut (24) 1 1/2" wide strips [(16) 1 1/2" wide strips].

CORNER STONES:

From the background fabric, cut (2) 3 1/2" wide strips [(1) 3 1/2" wide strip]. Subcut the strips [strip] into (16) 3 1/2" squares. Cut the 3 1/2" squares diagonally in both directions to create (64) quarter-square triangles. From the contrasting fabric, cut (2) 8" wide strips [(2) 8" wide strips]. Subcut the strips into (16) 5" x 8" rectangles [(16) 5" x 8" rectangles].

SEWING THE SASHING STRIPS

To the long edges of the 2 1/2" background strips, sew the 1 1/2" contrasting strips. Be very careful that you maintain a 1/4" seam allowance. You might test your stitching before you begin. You will have (12) 4 1/2" strip-set units that appear as in figure 1.

(figure 1)

Carefully press (don't iron) your seams to the outer contrasting fabric. Ironing causes the strip units to "smile" and you need them to stay as straight as possible. Therefore, very carefully press the seams. Ironing is a back-and-forth motion. Pressing is an up-and-down motion. Save the ironing for shirts!

Subcut each of the strip-set units into (2) 18 1/2" x 4 1/2" sashing pieces. You will have (24) sashing pieces. Set aside until you've made the corner stones.

NOTE: The length of these sashing pieces should be cut the same as the squared-up size of your appliqué block. In other words, if your blocks are trimmed to 17 1/2" for a 17" finished size, then your sashing strips should be 17 1/2" long.

SEWING THE CORNER STONES

(See figure 2.)

(figure 2)

So that the edges of the corner stone blocks are on the straight-of-grain, the "ribbons" must be cut on the bias. Cut the (16) 5" x 8" rectangles into 2" bias strips as shown in figure 3, represented by the solid lines. The center strip will be slightly wider than 2 inches. Just make sure that both cuts for the center strip start at the corner.

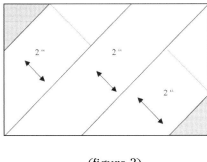

(figure 3)

You may discard the triangles that are shown in gray (figure 3) and use them in another project someday. From each of the 5" x 8" rectangles you will be left

with (3) strips, one long and two shorter. Trim one end of each of the two shorter strips as shown in figure 3 and represented by the dashed line. Discard the triangles you've cut or use them in another project someday.

Sew (2) quarter-square triangles from the background fabric to one of the shorter strips you created from the 5" x 8" rectangles as shown in figure 4. The only edges that you need to line up are the ones as shown. Repeat, using all of the quarter-square triangles and short bias strips. You should have (32) of these units. Press the seams to the contrasting fabric strip in the center, taking care not to distort the unit. (Press, don't iron!)

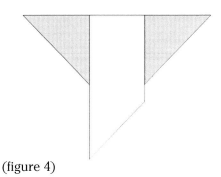

(figure 4)

Your next step is to sew these units to the (16) longer bias strips that you cut from the 5" x 8" rectangles. Be very careful to line up the contrast strips from the units you've made so that it appears to be one solid

piece overlapping another solid piece. The picture (figure 5) should help you. Again, press to the contrasting fabric strips, being very careful not to distort the unit.

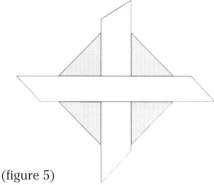

(figure 5)

Using your 6" square ruler, center the diagonal line on the long bias strip. Align the 2 1/4" markings (in both directions) over the innermost corner of two of the adjacent triangles. With your rotary cutter, trim the block on the two sides that contain the triangles on which you've centered the square ruler. Rotate the block and repeat on the other two sides. You should have a block that looks like the image in (figure 2) and that measures 4 1/2" x 4 1/2".

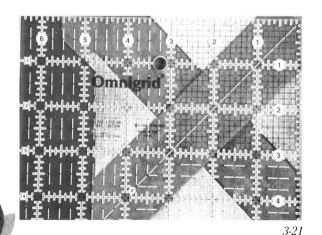

3-21

Repeat the above detailed steps until you have a total of (16) 4 1/2-inch blocks. Now you're ready to put it all together!

PUTTING IT ALL TOGETHER

Begin by making (4) sashing units that consist of (4) corner stones and (3) sashing strips each. Start with a corner stone block, add a sashing strip unit, then add another block, another sashing strip unit, another block, sashing strip unit and end with a corner stone block. See (figure 6) for placement. Press all the seams to the sashing strip unit. Repeat until you have (4) of these rows complete.

Arrange your appliqué blocks in a manner that is pleasing to you – three across and three down. For each of these three rows you will start with a sashing strip unit, add an appliqué block, add a sashing strip unit, an appliqué block, sashing strip unit, appliqué block and end with a sashing strip unit. Repeat until you have (3) of these rows completed. See (figure 6) for placement. Press all seams to the sashing.

You should have (4) sashing rows and (3) appliqué rows. To put it all together, start with a sashing row. Add an appliqué row, another sashing row, and another appliqué row, sashing row, appliqué row and end with the last sashing row. See (figure 6) for placement.

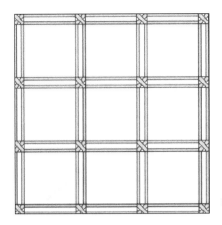

(figure 6)

Congratulations! You have now completed the center of your quilt! At this point you could stop, sandwich/baste it, quilt it and bind it. But wait! There's one more pattern. To make the complete quilt as designed, you'll want to add the appliqué border!

THE BORDER

To begin with, the appliqué pattern for the border requires that your border be about 11" wide by the length of your quilt top. Since everyone sews a little differently, my 1/4" seam allowance might be slightly different than your 1/4" seam allowance and your blocks a different size. This will make a difference to the measurement of your quilt top to this point. I recommend that you measure your quilt top once you have the sashing finished. That measurement plus 22" plus a few inches of extra play will give you the amount of fabric you'll need for your border. In other words, if your top at this point measures 70 1/2" x 70 1/2", add 22" for the width of the borders and then a

little extra for distortion from stitching. You will probably need about 95" of length. Cut your yardage into four strips the length of the fabric. If you are using a fabric that is more than 44" wide, you still need only cut your strips 11 or 12" wide.

Find the center of one of the strips and either finger press it or sew a running stitch with a contrasting thread to mark the center.(3-22) You can set the border strips aside as you prepare your appliqué.

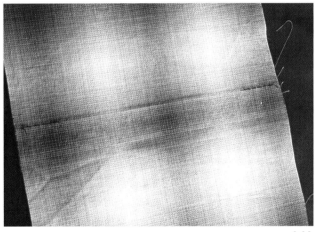

3-22

To make the clear vinyl overlay, I made a single tracing of the swag pattern. Be sure that you include all the center markings. For instructions, see "Placement" on page 12. The other thing that I found helpful was to make a mark along the bottom edge of the swag overlay, 1" from the lowest point of the swag. This line was matched up to the raw edge of my border fabric.(3-23) Now I knew exactly where to put the swag so that the three lined up evenly along the length of the border as well as from the outside edges.

I traced the swag pattern onto the non-shiny side of my freezer paper. Appliqué pieces #1 and #2 were traced together as a single unit. Actually, I traced half the pattern. I folded my piece of freezer paper, right sides together, stapled the two layers and then cut both layers at once. This way I was sure that both ends of the swag were identical. The sets of cross-hatching along the line that separates the top from the bottom are placement registers. When sewing the top and bottom halves of the swag back together, the bias of the fabric will make it very easy to stretch and get the pieces misaligned. By matching these points, I was assured of less distortion. After ironing the

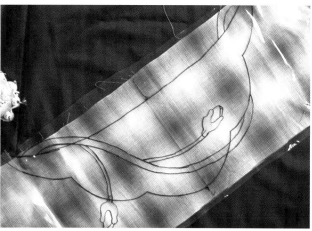

3-23

pattern onto the right side of the appliqué fabric and tracing the pattern, I extended the cross-hatching into the seam allowance to aid in placement later when the freezer paper template would be removed and the lines would no longer be there.

Go ahead and trim your seam allowance all around appliqué piece #2, but don't trim the seam allowance from the top edge of #1. This extra fabric will give you something to hold and to pin #2 onto. Once you have stitched #2 to #1, you will want to turn it over and trim the excess seam allowance to 3/16".

To place the swag appliqué onto the background, line up the center markings on the swag to the center markings you made on the border strip. My center fold on the template made a perfect center mark! You will be stitching the center of the three swags first. Remember, the lowest point of the center of the swag (the turn under line) is 1" from the raw edge of the border strip. The ends of the swag will be about 1 1/4" from the top raw edge. Stitch the swag to the background, but leave the seam open at the places marked on the pattern. This will let you tuck the ends of the vines in when you stitch them later.

If you are planning to hand quilt your *Prairie Album* you will want to trim away the background from behind the swag appliqué before adding your vines. Just be extra careful at the spots you have left open to tuck vine ends into later. I made my vines by cutting 1" wide bias strips and making 1/2" bias tape with my Clover Bias Tape Maker. I used the 1/4" Bias Tape Maker to make the stems for the buds. Because the curve is so sharp for the vine that is represented by piece #3, I used a template instead of bias tape. Too much fabric had to be eased into the inside curve of piece #3 that it appeared to be gathered. Making a template eliminated this problem. Remember to clip the inside curves before stitching.

When your center swag is in place, you will be able to place the other two with no problems. The ends of the swags meet but do not overlap. You do not need to "finish" the ends of the swags, as the ends will be covered by a ruched rose each time. Your rose will overlap part of the sashing as well, so you won't be able to add the roses until the border strips are attached to the quilt top.

The buds on the vines are made the same way that you did in Block #2, "Rose Spiral." In fact, if you still have the freezer paper templates, you can reuse them for the border instead of making new ones! The corner swag designs need to be appliquéd after the border strips are sewn to the quilt top. Because I used a plaid and did not want to worry about matching the plaid, I made my border with a long horizontal border style. However, if I had used any other fabric, I probably would have made mitered corners. The miter seam would have been mostly hidden behind the corner swag appliqué.

Once all the appliqué on the border strips was complete, I measured the strips, trimmed them to size and sewed them to the quilt top. With the border attached I appliquéd the corner swag designs. Again, the crosshatch markings aided in placement. Use the same principles for piecing the appliqué that you have throughout the quilt top.

When you are ready to place the ruched roses in the corners, I think you'll find as I did, that one flower would not cover that corner. So I ended up making a cluster of three roses. Use your favorite method for making the roses as described in "How do I Ruche Thee…" beginning on page 19.

Now you are ready to sandwich your top with the batting and backing to the quilt. Don't forget to trim away any background from behind the appliqué that will hinder your hand quilting stitch.

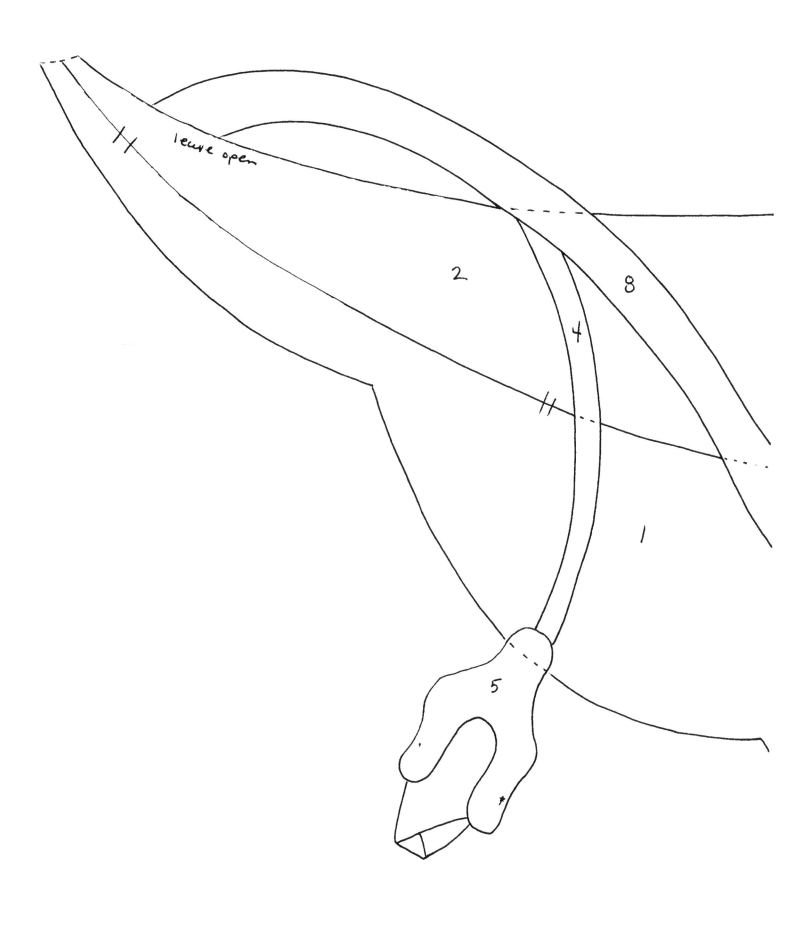

leave open

2

8

4

1

5

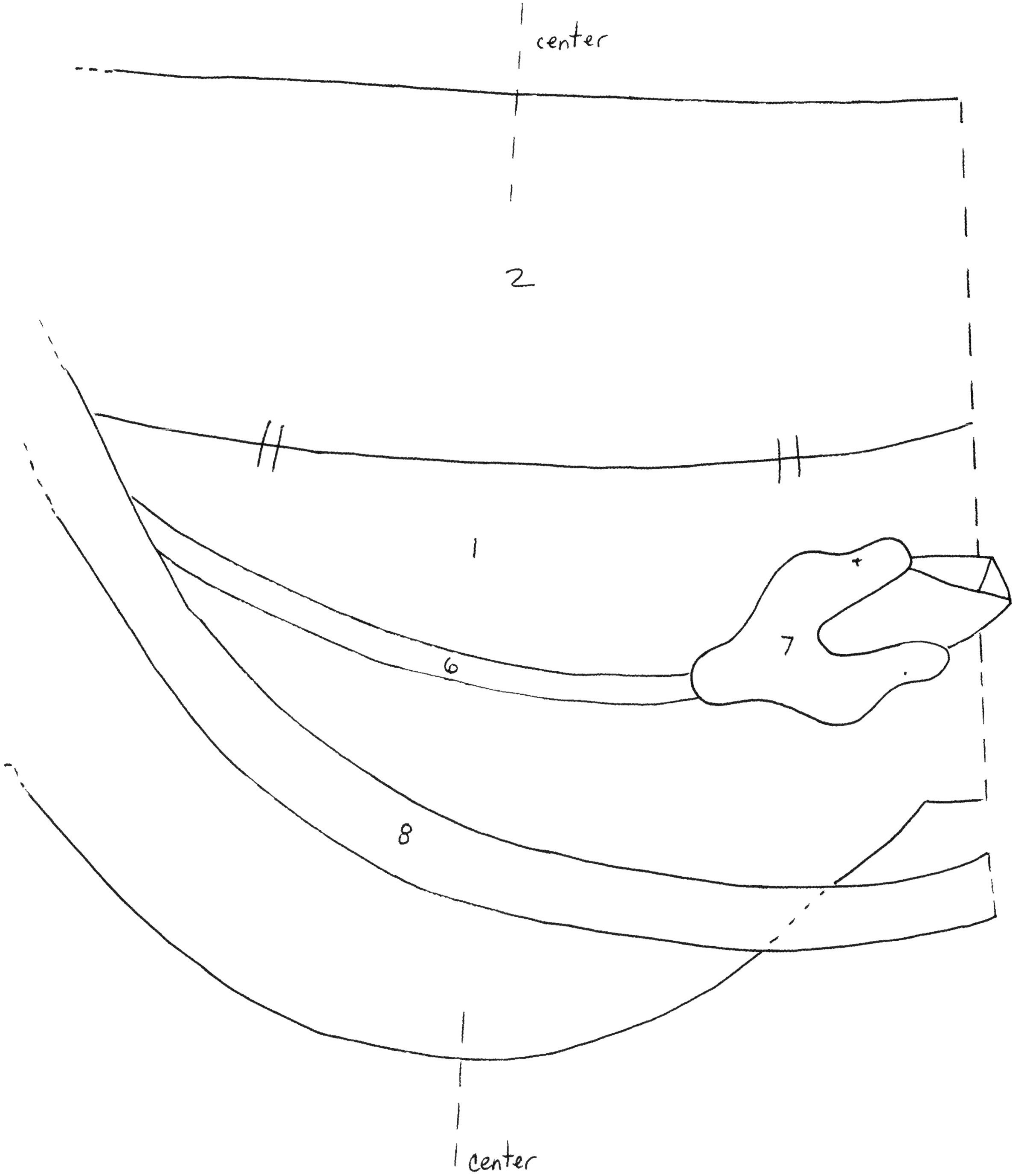

center

2

1

6

7

8

center

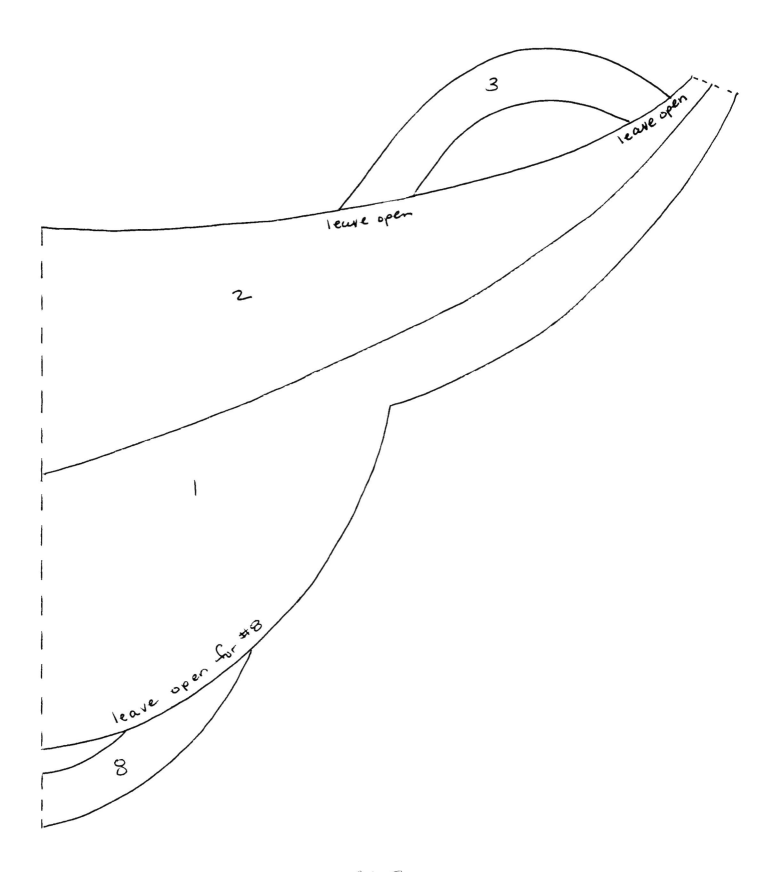

3

leave open

2

leave open

1

leave open for #8

8

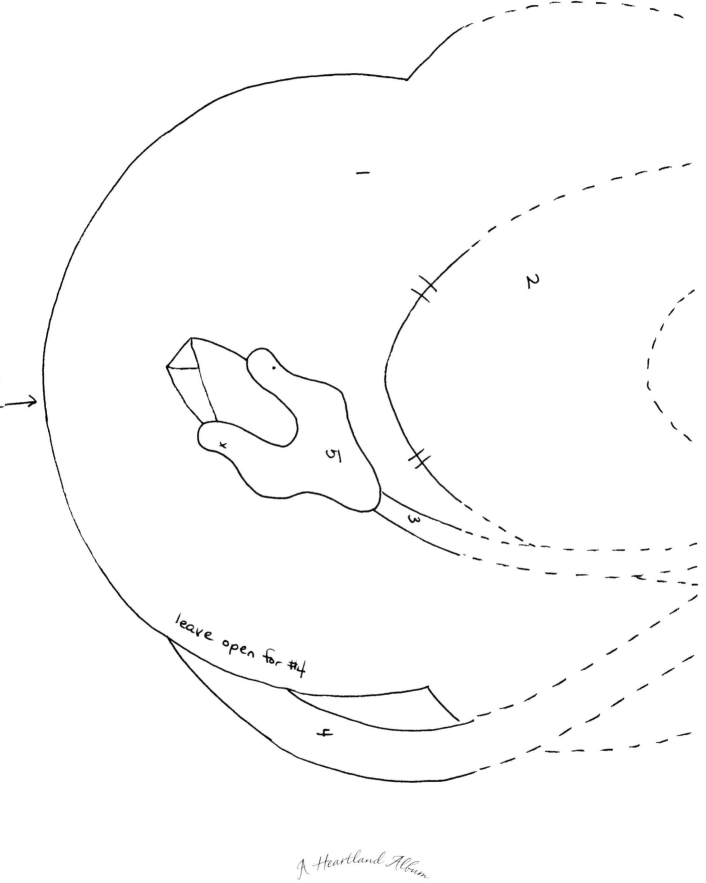

center

leave open for #4

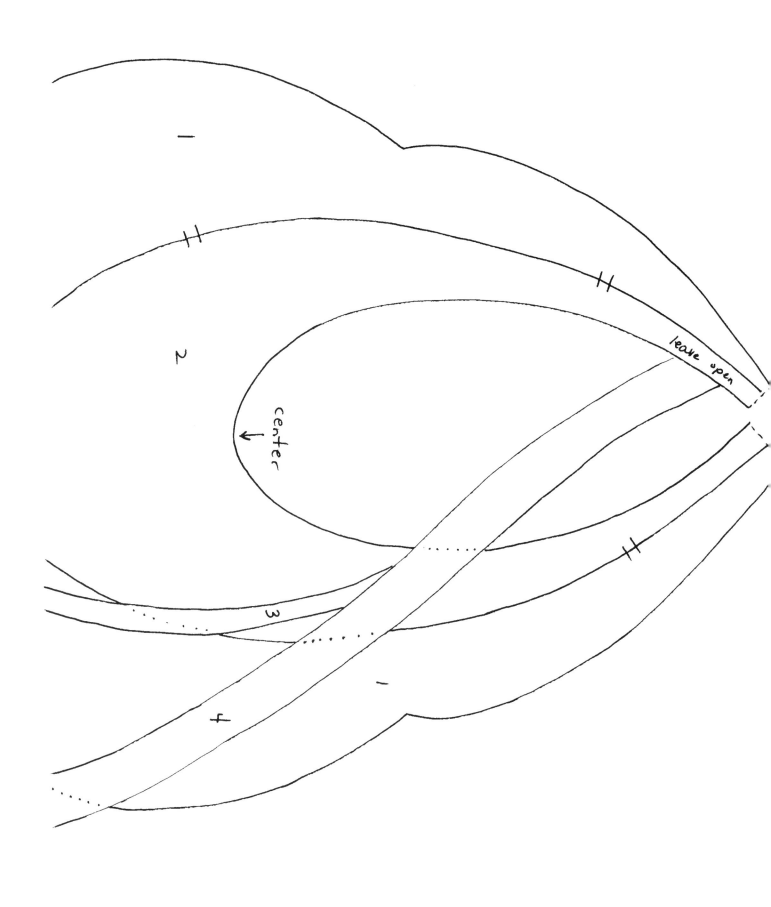

BORDER ALTERNATIVES

When you have completed the sashing on your *Prairie Album*, you may wish to call your quilt top finished. The sashing frames the appliqué blocks and can be considered complete without adding any other borders.

However, if you would like to make your quilt top larger, an additional border would certainly fill the bill. The appliquéd border patterns included within these pages frames the center nicely, but you may wish to do something different – something totally unique to you. Adding an original border will make the quilt more your own creation, and I really encourage that!

When trying to design a border that will enhance the rest of the quilt top and not look as if we just stuck something on the edges to make it bigger, we often are faced with the question, "What do I do?" I encourage you always to take elements from within the quilt top and incorporate them into the border, whether it is a pieced border or an appliquéd border design. When I designed my border, I brought the buds from Block #2, "Spiral Rose," to the border swags, as well as the ruched flowers from several of the blocks.

On this page are two other examples of appliquéd border designs. Kathy Berner of Prairie Village, Kan, in her *Prairie Adventure*, revisited Block #1, "Open Bud-Wreath," for the elements of her border. She didn't feel compelled to fill the entire border with appliqué, which served nicely to continue that open, clean feeling of her quilt top.*(3-24)*

Dorothy Stalling of Lenexa, Kan., in her rendition of *Prairie Album*, chose to pull flowers from several of the blocks to enhance her quilt top. Even though each of these flowers would not appear on the same stems in nature, she didn't let that fact hinder her design. The elements from the center of the quilt top, brought out to the edge of her quilt top serve to tie the two parts of the quilt top together very nicely. *(3-25)*

3-24

3-25

Projects

Prairie Flowers in Wool
by Nancy Nunn, Bonner Springs, Kan.
18"x 18"

Prairie Flower in Wool - Pillow

Fabric Requirements

Background:

18" x 18" square black wool

Appliqué: (sample uses hand dyed wools)

9" x 12" deep rose (appliqué pieces #7 and #9)

5" x 6" medium rose #1 (appliqué pieces #5)

5" x 6" medium rose #2 (appliqué pieces #6)

5" x 10" dark green (appliqué pieces #1 and #3)

4" x 7" light green (appliqué pieces #2 and #4)

2" x 8" brown and black plaid (appliqué pieces #8 and #11)

Pillow backing:

18" x 18" square coordinating print

You will also need:

Embroidery floss to match the appliqué wools

#7 Embroidery needle

Craft fiberfill

Begin by tracing the pattern for block #7, "Prairie Flower," onto an 18" x 18" square of clear upholstery vinyl. Be sure that you include all the center markings. For complete instructions, see "Placement" on page 12.

When working with wool, you will not be turning under a seam allowance, and in this project, you will go one step further away from needleturn by fusing the wool shape to your background before stitching. Trace the shapes onto the paper side of a light paper-backed fusible webbing. Unless you trace the mirror image of the pattern, your finished design will be the mirror image of the pattern. (Note that the sample does not include the tiny circles, #10.) Cut out the shape about 1/2" outside the line. Following the

written instructions that came with the product that you purchased, fuse the webbing to the wrong side of the appliqué wool. (Note that not all fusible webs use the same method for fusing. One will call for steam while another strongly advises against steam.) Cut out the shape on the line and then peal the paper backing away from the shape. Fuse the appliqué shapes to the background square, in the sequence as described by the numbering on the pattern. Again, be sure to follow the written instructions that came with your product.

Once all of the appliqué shapes are fused in place, you will stitch around each shape using the buttonhole stitch, as described in Buttonhole Stitch Appliqué on page 41. The sample pillow shown used two strands of embroidery floss, matching in color to the appliqué fabrics. You may, however, wish to use #8 Perle Coton. The Perle Coton is a little shinier and a thicker fiber than the floss. You might wish to experiment to get the look you favor.

When you have completed the appliqué, sew the wool block to your pillow backing fabric, right sides together, using a 1/4" seam allowance. Begin 6" before a corner, backstitch to secure, and sew all around the perimeter, ending with a backstitch 6" after the last corner. Clip the excess seam allowance from the corners of the square at a 45-degree angle to eliminate some of the bulk. Turn the pillow form right side out and stuff your form with a craft fiberfill, paying particular attention to the corners. When you have stuffed the form to your liking, whipstitch the opening closed with a thread that matches the pillow front (our sample is black) and your pillow is complete.

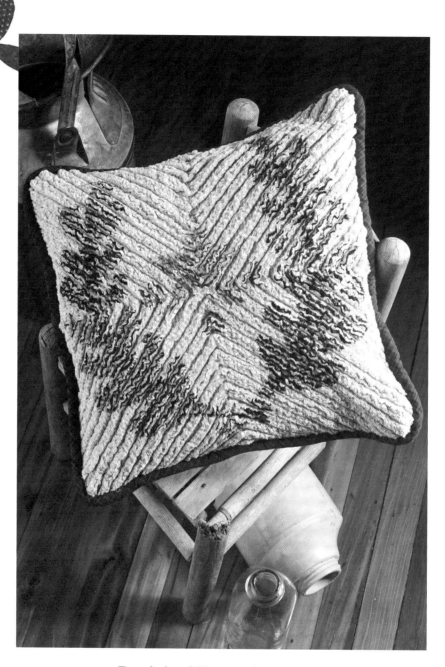

Prairie Album Chenille
by Pat Moore, Kansas City, Kan.
16"x 16"

Prairie Album Chenille - Pillow

Fabric Requirements

Chenille front:

    1 yard light homespun plaid

    1/4 yard dark green homespun plaid

    1 fat quarter red homespun plaid

    6" x 6" square gold homespun plaid

Pillow back and piping:

    1/2 yard red plaid

You will also need:

    2 yards 3/8" piping chord

    16" pillow form

Begin by tracing the pattern for block #6, "Faith," onto an 18" x 18" square of clear upholstery vinyl. Be sure that you include all the center and side center markings. For complete instructions, see "Placement" on page 12.

Chenille begins with several layers of fabrics. Very interesting effects can be obtained by varying the sequence of the layers. You might use some scraps before making your pillow and experiment to see what you like the best. The sample shows the appliqué layer as the second one down. However, the design might be less subtle if it is the third layer down, and it would change again if you made the appliqué on the first layer.

Trace the appliqué shapes onto the non-shiny side of freezer paper. Through the center of the pattern draw a few straight lines, both horizontal and vertical, through the leaf fronds that will represent the straight grain of the fabric.

Your vinyl will help you see exactly where. With a dry iron, set on the wool setting, iron the freezer paper templates onto the right side of your fabrics. It is important that you align the markings you made with the straight grain of the fabrics. Unlike the reverse appliqué technique used in the *Prairie Album* quilt, you will need a template for the veins (template piece #1a). Trace the shape onto the fabric and gently remove the templates. Cut the shapes out on the traced lines. You will not need any seam allowance for this project.

Cut the yard of light homespun into (4) fat quarters. Layer the fat quarters, one on top of the other, and right sides up. Decide where you want to place the appliqué shapes. For the sample, we place them between the top fat quarter layer and the next one down. Place a few pins through the layers to prevent slipping while you stitch. The secret to the Chenilling process is to stitch the rows on the bias. For our pillow, we stitched the channels as in figure 1.

Figure 1

We began by marking the center with an "X" on the top layer with a water-soluble marking pen, represented by the dashed line in Figure 1. Centering the "X" on the fat quarter means that you will have a little excess at the top and the bottom. The excess may be removed later or you may wish to trim the fat quarter to 18" x 18."

Stitch through all layers 1/4" from the drawn line, crossing no line and crossing no stitching. You will end up with four chevron designs all pointing to the center. From each stitching line, stitch another line 1/2" away. Continue stitching, leaving 1/2" between each row of stitching until you have filled the entire surface.

With scissors or a rotary cutter designed for the purpose, cut through three of the four layers of fabric between each of the rows of stitching. Try to keep the cut evenly spaced within each of the rows. You **WILL NOT** cut through the very bottom layer. If you do have an accident and cut through the bottom later, you may repair the slit by ironing a little piece of fusible interfacing to cover the slit from the wrong side. This will act as a bandage and keep the hole from showing from the front. When all the rows of stitching have been cut, put the block into the washing machine with cool water to agitate and then place into the dryer to tumble

dry. Be sure to use cool water so you don't permanently set the water-soluble marking pen. The washing and the drying will make the rows "bloom" and the chenilling will take effect. If the bloom isn't to your liking, you may need to repeat the agitation and drying steps so that the blooming is fluffier. Because you made your cuts through the fabric on the bias, the washing and drying will not cause the fabric to ravel, but to curl. This is why you take such care to place the appliqué on the grain of the fabric to align with the straight of grain of the fat quarters.

Square your block with a rotary cutter, rotary cutting ruler and mat to a 16" x 16" square.

From the 1/2 yard of red plaid, cut (1) 16 1/2" x 11 1/2" rectangle and (1) 16 1/2" x 13" rectangle. Set these aside for now.

From the remainder of the 1/2 yard of red plaid, cut enough 2" bias strips to sew together, end-to-end, resulting in a 72" long bias strip. The longer the strips are, the fewer of them will be needed to reach 72". I think the fewer seams, the better.

With your zipper foot put in place on your sewing machine, fold the bias strip around the 3/8" chording and sew right next to the chording, making the piping to finish your pillow edge.*(3-26)*

Beginning on the bottom edge of your chenille block, sew the piping to the raw edge of the block all the way around on the right side of the block, matching the raw edges. You will need to clip into the seam allowance of the piping to go around the corners. (3-27) When you reach the beginning with your piping, you may tightly cross over the ends to finish (raw ends will end up hidden in the seam allowance) or you can cut the excess chording, butting the ends together, and finishing the bias as you would a binding.

Retrieve the rectangles that you set aside. Beginning with the 16" x 11 1/2" rectangle, fold one of the 16" edges 1/4" and press. Turn under another 1/4" and sew to finish. Turn under one of the 16" edges of the other rectangle 1/4" and press and then turn under 1 1/2" and sew along the folded edge to finish. With right sides together, layer the 16" x 13" rectangle, matching the raw edges. With right sides together, layer the 16" x 11" rectangle matching the other raw

edges. You will notice that the hemmed edges of the rectangles overlap over the center of the block. With your zipper foot in place, sew through all layers, right next to the piping. Trim the corners to eliminate some of the bulk. Turn the "envelope" and your pillow is finished. All that remains is for you to stuff the pillow with the 16" pillow form. If the form doesn't completely fill your pillow, you might consider stuffing the corners with a little fiberfill.

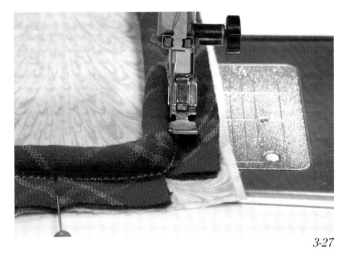

3-27

3-26

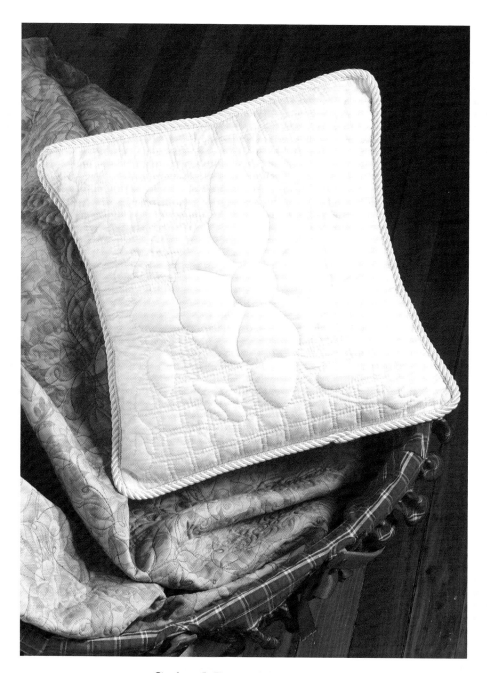

Spiral Rose Trapunto
by Kathy Delaney, Overland Park, Kan.
14"x 14"

Fabric Requirements:

1/2" yard solid fabric for pillow top and
   pillow back

18" square medium-high loft batting for
   Trapunto

18" square low loft batting for quilting

Fat quarter muslin for pillow top backing

You will also need:

Basting thread to contrast with the solid
   pillow-top fabric

Quilting thread to match the solid pillow-
   top fabric

Decorator chording to match the solid
   pillow-top fabric

14" pillow form

Using a light box so that you can easily see, trace the pattern onto the right side of a 15" x 15" square of the solid pillow-top fabric with a water-soluble marking pen. I chose Block #2, "Rose Spiral," for my pillow.

Following the directions in "Trapunto" beginning on page 43, prepare your pillow top. I quilted around each of the design shapes as well as quilting a double crosshatch grid in the background.

Before constructing my pillow, I washed the water-soluble marker out of the top with cool water and then blocked to square. I thought the dryer might distort my pillow top. Cotton quilting thread seems to shrink just a bit when washed for the first time. This aided in the Trapunto effect of my pillow top. Your quilted pillow top may measure about 14" square after washing.

To the right side of the pillow top and beginning at the center of the bottom edge, sew the decorator chording to the edge, matching the raw edge of the pillow to the edge of the tape. I use my zipper foot so that I can sew right next to the chording. Tightly over-lap the ends, crossing them toward the raw edge and stitch. The ends will be hidden in the seam allowance.

From the remainder of the 1/2 yard of solid fabric, cut two 11" x 14" rectangles. Along one of the 14" edges of each of the rectangles, turn under the fabric 1/4" and press. Turn under again 1/4" and sew to finish. With right sides together, layer the rectangles onto the pillow top, matching the raw edges to the edges of the pillow top. The hemmed edges will overlap across the center.

Sew all the way around the pillow, right next to the chording. Trim the corners to eliminate some of the bulk. All that is left to complete your pillow is to turn the envelope and stuff with a 14" pillow form.

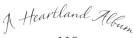

Whispers
by Kathy Delaney, Overland Park, Kan.
Quilted by Jeanne Zyck
62"x 62"

Fabric Requirements:

(I used at least 16 different fabrics from various lines designed by Robyn Pandolf for Moda Fabrics. You may wish to use a variety of 30's reproductions or some other collections of pastel fabrics. The design will work as well with darker fabrics or brighter prints, perhaps batiks.)

3 3/4 yards background for blocks, sashing, and border (You might have noticed that I used two different background fabrics; one for the blocks and one for the sashing and border.)

1/2 yard cuts of 5-6 fabrics for Celtic bias (blocks), sashing and border swags

(10) Fat quarters of coordinating fabrics for appliqué and sashing

1 yard fabric for the Celtic Heart Rope in the border

4 yards backing fabric

72" x 72" piece of batting

1/2" yard fabric for binding

You will also need:

1/4" Bias Tape Maker for appliqué stems

3/8" Bias Tape Maker for Celtic Heart border

1/8" Celtic bar

Template plastic

To make *Whispers* I chose Blocks #1 ("Open-Bud Wreath"), #2 ("Spiral Rose"), #3 ("Hot Poker Vine") and #5 ("Tulip Wreath"). I think these four blocks were the most conducive to the Celtic appliqué process. I look for patterns that are simpler when I want to add the accent Celtic tubes. Follow the directions described in "Celtic Appliqué" beginning on page 45 to make your blocks.

When your blocks are complete, turn them right side down onto a clean terry cloth towel and press. Using a rotary cutter, rotary ruler and mat, square the blocks to 18" x 18". Be sure that you center the appliqué. I trimmed my blocks 9" from either side of the center markings, both horizontally and vertically. Even though the blocks were pressed before trimming, the finger pressing, though faint, was still visible enough for me to see where the center lay.

From the fabrics you used for your appliqué, cut (24) 1 1/2" x 18" strips. From your background fabric cut (12) 1 1/2" x 18" strips. Sew an appliqué fabric strip on either side of the background strips with a 1/4" seam allowance. You should have (12) strips sets that measure 3 1/2" x 18". Press the seam allowances to the appliqué fabric strips. (See figure 1)

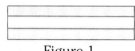

Figure 1

From your appliqué fabrics cut (36) 1 1/2" x 1 1/2" squares. From your background cut (45) 1 1/2" x 1 1/2" squares. With these squares you will make (9) Nine-Patch blocks that will measure 3 1/2" x 3 1/2," using (4) appliqué fabric squares and (5) background fabric squares for each Nine-Patch block. Press the row seams to the center to that they are opposite the strip sets, making matching the seams easier. I mixed up the fabrics and tried not to repeat fabrics so that each of the Nine-Patch blocks was different. I did not always succeed, but I don't think they detract. (See Figure 2)

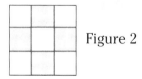

Figure 2

Sew a Nine-Patch block to one end of (7) of the strip sets (See Figure 3) and both ends of (1) of the strip sets. (See Figure 4) Press the seam allowance toward the strip set.

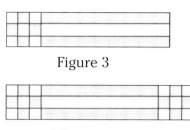

Figure 3

Figure 4

Decide in what order you want your blocks to be sewn together. Number the blocks, left to right, 1-4 starting in the upper left and ending in the lower right.

Sew a strip set to the left side of each of the appliquéd blocks. (See Figure 5) Press the seam allowance to the strip set.

Figure 5

Sew a Figure 3 unit to the top of each of the appliqué blocks (Nine-Patch on the left), to the bottom of Blocks #3 and #4 (Nine-Patch on the left) and to the right side of Block #2 (Nine-Patch on the top). Sew a Figure 4 unit to the right side of Block #4. Press all the seams to the strip sets. Sew the (4) Block units together to complete the center of your quilt. The opposing seams should fit together so that all your seams will intersect neatly.

THE BORDER

At this point, you could stop, quilt your quilt and bind it as it stands now. However, you may wish to add a border that includes a Celtic Heart Rope design.

Measure through the center of your quilt top to determine the length of your border. Mine measured 44 1/2" x 44 1/2". From your border fabric, cut (4) strips 10 1/2" x 67+". (I always cut my borders longer and then trim to fit once I have completed the appliqué.)

Using the placement overlay vinyl and freezer paper templates from the *Prairie Album* border (see page 97 for how I made the placement overlay, and page 98 for the templates) make the appliqué pieces for the border swags. This time I did not use the corner swag patterns. (See page 98 for appliqué piecing instructions regarding the border swags.) I used different fabrics for each of my border swags. Feel free to choose fabrics according to your own tastes. Unlike the full *Prairie Album* quilt, I only had room for two swags on a side in this quilt. Find the center of the border strip and place one end of the swag right next to the center point. Use the vinyl overlay for placement in relation to the outside edge. Stitch two swag units to each of the border strips.

Trace the Celtic Heart border template found on pages 120 and 121 onto a piece of template plastic and carefully cut out with paper scissors. Be sure to include the tabs as they are shown. These tabs will help you center the template on the border swags to mark the bias tape appliqué.

From the 1-yard piece of fabric for the Celtic Heart Rope, cut 3/4" bias strips. You will want the strips to be as long as possible so I suggest that you cut them from the center of the piece of fabric. You may need about 12 of the strips. With your 3/8" Bias Tape Maker, prepare the bias tape. Be sure to store the prepared bias tape on empty bathroom tissue or paper towel cores to keep the crease from relaxing and eliminate the possibility of wrinkling your bias tape.

Center the template on a swag appliqué and lightly trace just the hearts. The tabs are just for placement purposes. The bars between the hearts represent the bias tape. I just traced the top edge of the bars and then I was sure to cover the line with the appliqué so it did not show. You only need the outside edge of the hearts and the upper edge of the bars to help you place the bias tape.

3-28

to that measurement, centering the appliqué. Sew the two strips to the right and left sides of the quilt top. Measure your quilt top again, horizontally, and cut the remaining two strips to that measurement, centering the appliqué. Sew the strips to the top and bottom of your quilt top. The last step is to make ruched flowers (using the method of your choice) to cover the raw edges of the swags. (See "How Do I Ruche Thee…" on page 19.) The flowers will cover an edge of the Nine-Patches in the sashing.

Beginning on the left side of the swag, place the bias tape onto the border and follow the line you traced all the way around from one heart to the next. Notice that you will need to travel the bias tape under the tape at the top intersection. Study the photograph of the Celtic Heart knot to see how the rope is placed.*(3-28)*

An alternative would be to miter the corners. In this case, you will need the equivalent to the width of the borders added to both ends of the borders to allow for the miter.

Use your favorite method to quilt your top and bind it and you are done with your *Whispers* wall hanging.

If your bias tape becomes too short to go all the way around the heart, cut it at the place where the rope overlaps it. A break in the bias will never show as a break when it is behind the bias in the "knot." *(3-29)*

When all of the Celtic Heart Rope has been appliquéd in place you are ready to sew your borders to the quilt center. Measure your quilt top, vertically, through the center. Cut two of the border strips

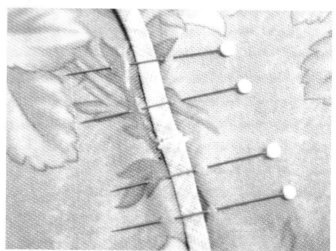

3-29

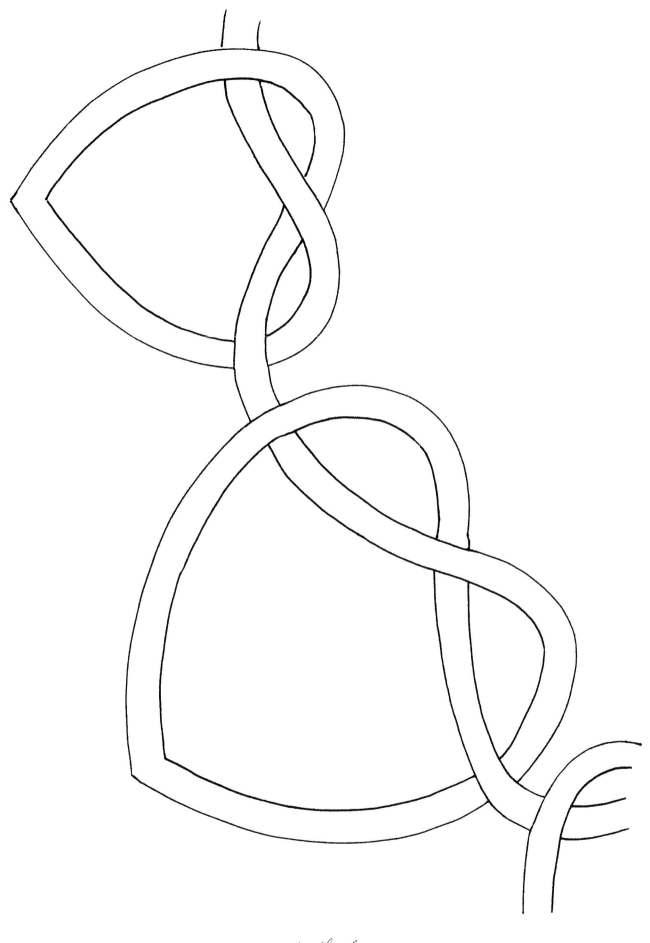

Prairie Album
by Kathy Delaney, Overland Park, Kan.
Quilted by Jeanne Zyck
93"x 93"

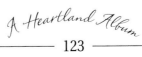

Geraldine's Prairie Album
by Geraldine Strader, Kansas City, Kan.
93"x 93"

Redwork Table Runner
by Carol Kirchoff, Overland Park, Kan.
22 1/2"x 50"

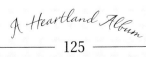

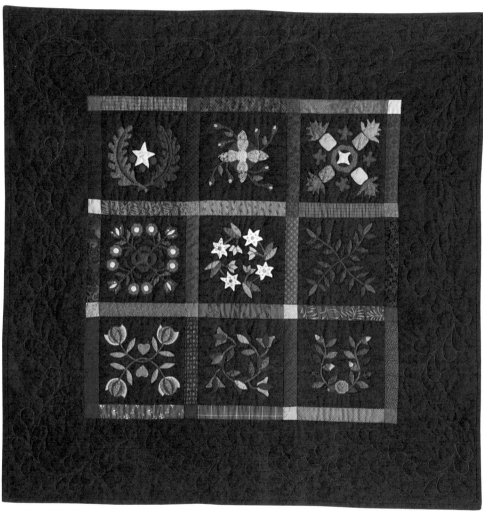

Mini Album
by Linda Mooney, Shawnee, Kan.
35"x 35"

Prairie Sampler
by Michele Sieben, Shawnee, Kan.
Quilted by Rosie Mayhew
93"x 93"

Prairie Adventure
by Kathy Berner, Prairie Village, Kan.
Quilted by Lyn Zeh
77"x 77"

Ring Around the Rosy
by Donna Howard, Watertown, S.D.
52"x 52"

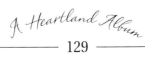

Prairie Salsa
by Tresa Jones, Seneca, Kan.
Quilted by Kelly Ashton
76"x 76"

Little Flowers on the Prairie
by Cathy Smith, Overland Park, Kan.
58"x 58"

Hearts and Flowers: Hand Applique from Start to Finish
Kansas City Star Books
1729 Grand
Kansas City, Mo. 64108
816-234-4402 and say "Books"
www.PickleDish.com

Moda Fabrics, Kinkame Silk Threads
United Notions
13795 Hutton Dr.
Dallas, Tx. 75234
972-484-8901 FAX: 972-241-2932

Richard Hemming Needles, John James Needles
Colonial Needle Company
74 Westmoreland Ave.
White Plains, NY 10606
914-946-7474 FAX: 914-946-7002

Bias Tape Maker
Clover Needlecraft, Inc.
1007 E. Dominguez St., #L
Carson, Ca. 90746-3620
310-516-7846   FAX: 310-516-1528

RucheMark Circular Ruching Guide
Thimbleworks
P.O. Box 462
Bucyrus, Oh. 44820
419-562-650 FAX: 419-562-6733

Bias Bars
Celtic Design Company
P.O. Box 2643
Sunnyvale, Ca. 94087-0643

Omnigrid
(A Division of Prym/Dritz)
P.O. Box 5028
Spartanburg, SC 29304
864-587-5269   FAX: 864-587-3322

Index of Patterns

Here is a chronological list — including repeats — of the quilt patterns and designs published by The Kansas City Star from 1928 through 2002. If you'd like to see the patterns on the pages of the newspaper, microfilm copies of The Star are available at the Kansas City Public Library's Main Branch, 311 E. 12th St., Kansas City, Mo.

For an alphabetical list of the designs, see Wilene Smith's Quilt Patterns: An Index to The Kansas City Star Patterns (details in Bibliography). For a thumbnail sketch of each pattern, see Volume 5 of The Ultimate Illustrated Index to The Kansas City Star Quilt Pattern Collection by the Central Oklahoma Quilters Guild (details in Bibliography). Months not listed here had no published quilt patterns.

1928
- September
  - Pine Tree
  - Album Quilt
- October
  - French Star
  - Log Cabin
  - Rob Peter and Pay Paul
  - Cherry Basket
  - Wedding Ring
- November
  - Jacob's Ladder
  - Greek Cross
  - Sky Rocket
  - Double T
- December
  - Ocean Wave
  - Wild Goose Chase
  - Old Maid's Puzzle
  - Rambler

1929
- January
  - Weathervane
  - Monkey Wrench
  - Spider Web
  - Irish Chain
- February
  - Rising Sun
  - Princess Feather
  - Double Nine Patch
  - Eight-Pointed Star
- March
  - Goose in the Pond
  - Dove in the Window
  - Beautiful Star

  - Broken Circle
  - Beggar Block
- April
  - Cupid's Arrow Point
  - Noon Day Lily
  - Lafayette Orange Peel
  - Necktie
- May
  - Duck and Ducklings
  - House on the Hill
  - Crossed Canoes
  - Turkey Tracks
- June
  - Ribbon Border Block
  - Posey
  - Bird's Nest
  - Crosses and Losses
  - Double Star
- July
  - Jack in the Box
  - Aircraft
  - Springtime Blossoms
  - Sunbeam
- August
  - Saw-Tooth
  - Cross and Crown
  - Hands All 'Round
  - Honey Bee
  - Flower Pot
- September
  - Susannah
  - Goose Tracks
  - Fish Block
  - Wedding Ring
- October
  - Swastika

  - Seth Thomas Rose
  - "V" Block
  - Little Beech Tree
- November
  - Palm Leaf
  - Tulip Applique
  - Mill Wheel
  - Order No. 11
  - Old King Cole's Crown
- December
  - Strawberry Block
  - Old King Cole
  - Little Wooden Soldier
  - Road to Oklahoma

(The "Santa's Parade Quilt" series ran in December 1929).

1930
- January
  - Churn Dash
  - Corn and Beans
  - Rose Cross
  - Milky Way
- February
  - True Lovers Buggy Wheel
  - Indiana Puzzle
  - Blazing Star
  - Aster
- March
  - Sunflower
  - Grape Basket
  - Steps to the Altar
  - Kaleidoscope

  - Dutchman's Puzzle
- April
  - English Flower Garden
  - Single Wedding Ring
  - Pin Wheels
  - Cross and Crown
- May
  - Missouri Puzzle
  - Merry Go-Round
  - Lone Star
  - Missouri Star
  - Sail Boat
- June
  - Virginia Star
  - Rail Fence
- July
  - Mexican Star
  - Basket of Oranges
  - Rose Album
  - Clay's Choice
- August
  - Maple Leaf
  - Sunbonnet Sue
  - Compass
  - Kaleidoscope
  - Rainbow Tile
- September
  - Goblet
  - Calico Puzzle
  - Broken Dishes
  - Swallows in the Window
- October
  - Secret Drawer
  - Spider Web
  - Marble Floor
  - Pinwheel

(The "Memory Bouquet
Quilt" series ran in
October 1930.)
- November
  Grandmother's Favorite
  Indian Emblem
  Friendship
  Puss in the Corner
  Sage-Bud
  (The "Memory Bouquet
  Quilt" series ran in
  November 1930).
- December
  Turnabout "T"
  Snow Crystals
  Sweet Gum Leaf
  Rose Dream

1931
- January
  Silver and Gold
  Tennessee Star
  Flower Pot
  Greek Cross
  Sheep Fold
- February
  Amethyst
  Wheel of Mystery
  Pontiac Star
  Baby Bunting
- March
  Seven Stars
  Rebecca's Fan
  French Bouquet
  Casement Window
- April
  Basket of Lilies
  King's Crown
  June Butterfly
  Fence Row
- May
  Indian Trail
  English Ivy
  Jackson Star
  Dutch Tulip
  Love Ring
- June
  Ararat
  Iris Leaf
  Ozark Diamond
  Kite Quilt
- July
  Cactus Flower

Arrowhead Star
Giddap
Sugar Loaf
- August
  Cross Roads
  Bachelor's Puzzle
  Morning Star
  Pineapple Quilt
  Dresden Plate
- September
  Stepping Stones
  Tennessee Star
  Chips and Whetstones
  Boutonniere
- October
  Prickly Pear
  Castle Wall
  Butterfly
  Pickle Dish
  Dutch Tile
- November
  Cottage Tulips
  Formosa Tea Leaf
  Bridge
  Evening Star
- December
  Poinsettia
  Goldfish
  Christmas Star
  Crazy Daisy

1932
- January
  Friendship Knot
  Circular Saw
  Heart's Desire
  Job's Tears
  Necktie
  (The "Horn of Plenty
  Quilt" series also ran
  in January 1932)
- February
  Autograph Quilt
  Hour-Glass
  Spring Beauty
  Grandmother's Basket
  (The "Horn of Plenty
  Quilt" series also ran
  in February 1932).
- March
  Grandmother's Favorite
  Quilting Design
  Shamrock

Magnolia Bud
- April
  Nose-Gay
  Diamond Field
  Red Cross
  Solomon's Puzzle
  "4-H" Club
- May
  Russian Sunflower
  Storm at Sea
  Crow's Nest
  Garden Maze
- June
  Cowboy's Star
  Ducklings
  Lend and Borrow
  Wheel of Fortune
- July
  Flying Bats
  Log Cabin
  Gretchen
  Double Nine Patch
  Kansas Star
- August
  Liberty Star
  Golden Glow
  Square Deal
  Purple Cross
- September
  Farmer's Wife
  Interlocked Squares
  Dove in the Window
  Florida Star

- October
  Interlocked Squares
  Pineapple Cactus
  Crazy Anne
  Old Missouri
  Clam Shells
  (A diagram of the
  "Happy Childhood Quilt"
      ran in October 1932.
- November
  Puss in the Corner
  Christmas Tree
  Christmas Toy Quilt
  Four Winds
  (The "Happy Childhood
  Quilt" also ran in
  October 1932.
- December
  Corner Posts

Snow Crystal
Pilot's Wheel
Christmas Tree
Star of Hope

1933
- January
  Star of Hope
  Old Spanish Tile
  Arkansas Star
  Star-shaped Quilting
    Design
  Floral Pattern Quilting
    Design
- February
  Sunflower Motif Quilting
    Design
  Petal and Leaf Quilting
    Design
  Medallion Quilting
    Design
  Pilot's Wheel

- March
  Arkansas Star
  Lone Star of Paradise
  Bouquet in a Fan
  Nest and Fledgling
- April
  St. Gregory's Cross
  Guiding Star
  Light and Shadow
  Flowing Ribbon
  Friendship Star
- May
  Broken Crown
  Square Within Square
  Oklahoma Sunburst
  Points and Petals
- June
  Square and Points
  Little Giant
  Puss in the Corner
  Double Arrow
- July
  Bridal Stairway
  Air-Ship Propeller
  Bridge Quilt
  Indian Canoes
  Flying Swallows
- August
  Double Pyramid
  Economy

Triplet
Jack in the Pulpit
• September
Broken Stone
Cypress
Cheyenne
Glory Block
• October
Square and Half Square
• November
Poinsettia
Ozark Trail
Four Crown
Crow's Nest
• December
Circle Upon Circle
Arkansas
Christmas Tree
Morning Glory
Charm Quilt

1934
• January
Star Center on French
Bouquet
Double Irish Chain
London Stairs
Franklin D. Roosevelt
• February
New Album
Valentine Quilt
Dogwood Blossom
Cat's Cradle
• March
Kansas Trouble
Water Glass
Eight Pointed Star
Broken Circle
Little Boy's Breeches
• April
Pin-Wheel
Jinx Star
Oklahoma Sunburst
Texas Pointer
• May
Snowball Quilt
Windmill Star
Flowering Nine-Patch
Joseph's Coat
• June
Christmas Tree
Lover's Lane
Crystal Star

Wagon Wheels
Friendship Quilt
• July
Triple Star
Gordian Knot
Red Cross
Airplane
• August
Japanese Garden
Feather Edge Star
Saw Tooth
Sunflower Design
Pattern
• September
Dogwood Design Pattern
Border and Block Design
Pattern
Lotus Leaf Design
Pattern
Whirling Pin Wheel
New Album
• October
Hazel Valley Cross
Roads
Jacob's Ladder
Arrow Star
Friendship Quilt
• November
Quilting Motif Design
Pattern
Square Design Pattern
Floral Motif Design
Pattern
Quilts and Gifts Design
Pattern
• December
Marble Quilt
Cluster of Lillies

1935
• January
Arabic Lattice
Coffee Cups
Fan Quilt
• February
Old-Fashioned String
Quilt
Arkansas Snowflake
Friday the 13th
Wedding Ring
• March
Missouri Daisy
Bridle Path

Farmer's Daughter
Arabic Lattice
• April
My Graduation Class
Ring
Goldfish
Ozark Trail
Tulip Quilt
• May
Grandmother's Basket
Churn Dash
Twinkle, Twinkle Little
Star
Indian Hatchet
Old Missouri
• June
String Quilt
Strawberry
Florida Star
Twinkle, Twinkle Little
Star
• July
Jacob's Ladder
Sonnie's Play House
Shaded Trail
Grandma's Brooch
Flower Basket
• August
Wind Mill
Diamond Circle
Railroad Crossing
Leaves and Flowers
Teapot
• September
Gold Bloom
Hands All Around
Apple Leaf
Four Leaf Clover
• October
Melon Patch
Arkansas Meadow Rose
Scrap Bag
Pine Cone
Album
• November
Squirrel in a Cage
Cog Wheels
Snail Trail
Compass and Chain
Broken Branch
• December
Basket of Flowers
Ozark Star

Shaded Trail
Kansas Dust Storm

1936
• January
Missouri Wonder
Flower of Spring
Circle Saw
Arrow Head
• February
Morning Star
White Lily
Seven Stars
Kansas Beauty
Young Man's Invention
• March
Wood Lily or Indian
Head
Star Sapphire
Pointing Star
IXL or I Excel
• April
Butterfly
Dove at the Window
Quilter's Pride
Martha Washington
• May
Dog Quilt
Patriotic Star
Ma Perkin's Flower
Garden
Cups and Saucers
Sickle
• June
Dove at the Window
Turkey Tracks
Jupiter Star
Lover's Link
• July
Hidden Star
Airport
Marble Quilt
• August
Anna's Pride
Star
• September
Whirligig Hexagon
Landon Sunflower
Chinese Puzzle
Rising Sun
• October
Ozark Cobblestone
Peggy Anne's Special

A Heartland Album

Happy Hunting Grounds
Mayflower
Dragonfly
• November
Basket of Diamonds
Mountain Road
Solomon's Temple
Rolling Stone
• December
Circle and Square
Grandmother's Tulip
Modern Broken Dish

1937
• January
The Kite
Arkansas Centennial
Flower Pot
Square Diamond
Whirling Star
• February
Nosegays
Four-Pointed Star
Golden Circle Star
• March
Right Hand of
Fellowship
Waves of the Sea
Spool Quilt
Old-Fashioned Goblet
Double "T"
• April
Quilt Without a Name
Dolly Madison
Ozark Tile
Star of Bethlehem
• May
Owl Quilt
Flower Garden Block
Depression
Diamond Cross
Winding Blade
Maple Leaf
• June
Album Quilt
Old Maid's Puzzle
Midget Necktie
• July
Flying Kite
Double Square
Indian Star
Russian Sunflower
• August

Ozark Sunflower
Hanging Basket
Basket of Diamonds
Broken Dish
• September
Verna Belle's Favorite
Broken Window
Old-Fashioned Quilt
Bear's Paw
Arrowhead
Necktie
• October
Modern Broken Dish
Clay's Choice
Winged Square
Quilting Design for
Many Quilts
Lotus Quilting Design
• November
Modified Floral
Quilting Design
Circular Quilting Design
Tulip Motif Quilting
Design
Conventional Quilting
Design
Favorite Quilting Design
• December
Motif Quilting Design
Household Quilting
Design

1938
• January
Quilt of Variety
Ladies' Aid Album
Old-Fashioned Wheel
• February
Electric Fan
• March
Border Quilting Design
Fair and Square
Texas Flower
• April
Twentieth Century Star
Broken Square
Letha's Electric Fan
• May
Jig Jog Puzzle
Bethlehem Star
Basket
Rebecca's Fan
North Star

Friendship Quilt
• June
Pin Wheel
Blockade
• July
Chinese Block
Little Boy's Breeches
Heart of the Home
• August
Versatile Quilting
Design
Friendship Quilt
Maple Leaf
• September
Double Cross
Friendship Quilt
• October
Six-Pointed Star
Flying "X"
• November
Contrary Husband
Floating Clouds
Right Hand of
Fellowship
White Square
• December
Wild Goose

1939
• January
Sandhills Star
• February
"T" Quilt
Small Wedding Ring
• March
Windmill
Wandering Flower
Pig Pen
• April
Farmer's Field
Sun Rays
• May
Swastika
Thrifty Wife
Crazy Tile
Chisholm Trail
• June
Lost Golsin'
Hexagon Beauty
Oak Grove Star
Pride of Ohio
• July
"X" Quartette

Double "T"
Rolling Stone
• August
Pine Burr
Corner Star
Broken Star
• September
Little Boy's Britches
Rosebud
Star and Box
Red Cross
• October
Our Country
Lost Paradise
Broken Path
• November
Crown of Thorns
Flag In, Flag Out
Buckeye Beauty
• December
Rosalia Flower Garden
Sylvia's Bow
Thrifty

1940
• January
Air Plane
Bluebell
Ladies' Fancy
• February
4-H
Six Point String
Little Cedar Tree
• March
Hicks Basket
Fan and Ring
• April
Silent Star
Cabin Windows
• May
Mother's Favorite Star
Comfort Quilt
Around the World
Flower Ring
• June
Mona's Choice
Long 9 Patch
Garden Walk
• July
The "X"
Double "V"
Whirl Around
• August

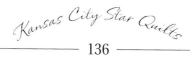

E-Z Quilt
Jig Saw Puzzle
Quilter's Fan
• September
Car Wheel
Winged Nine Patch
Spider Web
• October
Hexagon Star
Garden Patch
• November
Southside Star
• December
Carrie Nation
Spool Quilt
Springtime in the Ozarks
Four Patch Fox
and Goose

1941
• January
Colorado Quilt
Red Cross
• February
Mother's Choice
Cotton Boll
Anna's Choice
• March
Four Red Hearts
Arkansas Cross Roads
Arrowhead
• April
Seven Sisters
Whirling Star
Mosaic
• May
Missouri Sunflower
Fence Row
Wagon Wheels
• June
Fish Quilt
• July
May Basket
Periwinkle
Quint Five
"H" Square
• August
Starry Heavens
Friendship Chain
Flowers in a Basket
Contrary Wife
• September
Star Spangled Banner

1941 Nine Patch
Quilt in Light and Dark
• October
Four Buds
Radio Windmill
Four Leaf Clover
• November
Buzz Saw
Star of Alamo
Winding Blade
Kitchen Woodbox
• December
Friendship Ring
Whirling Five Patch
Old Indian Trail
Mexican Star

1942
• January
Sunlight and Shadows
Ice Cream Cone
Arrowheads
Molly's Rose Garden
• February
Tulips
Postage Stamp
Chain Quilt
• March
Four O' Clock
• April
Long Pointed Star
Victory Quilt
Victory Quilt in Another
Version
• May
Salute to the Colors
Ola's Quilt
Rosebud
Depression Quilt
• June
Airplane
Danish Stars
Signal Lights
Shepherd's Crossing
• July
London Stairs
Spider Web
Broken Sugar Bowl
• August
Thorny Thicket
Envelope Motif
• September
Red and White

Crisscross
Drunkard's Trail
All-Over Pattern of
Octagons
• October
Full Moon
Red Cross
• November
Ocean Wave
Modern Version of
String Quilt
Kansas Dugout
• December
Jerico Walls
Basket Quilt in
Triangles
Cornerstone
Pattern of Chinese
Origin

1943
• January
Turtle on a Quilt
Red-White-Blue Color
Scheme
Carrie's Favorite
Applique
• February
Quilting Design in
Points
Envelope
• March
Adaptations of the
Indian Trail
Builder's Block Quilt
• April
Salute to Loyalty
Octagons and Squares
• May
Evelyne's Whirling
Dust Storm
Army Star
• June
Broken Dish
Spider Web
• July
Mountain Peak
Four-Corner Puzzle
Texas Trellis
• August
Winding Blades
Reminiscent of the
Wedding Ring

• September
Ice Cream Cone
Whirling Pinwheel
Broken Wheel
• October
Fence Row
World Fair
• November
Lone Star
• December
Formal Flower Bed
Patchwork Cushion Top
Mowing Machine

1944
• January
Striped Plain Quilt
• February
Butterfly in Angles
Washington Stamp
• March
Whirling Blade
Jack in the Pulpit
Evening Star
• April
Friendship Name Chain
• May
Rosebud
President Roosevelt
New Four Pointer
• June
Sailboat Oklahoma
• July
Blue Blades Flying
• August
Soldier Boy
Seven Stars
Solomon's Puzzle
• September
Roads to Berlin
Envelope Quilt
Victory Boat
• October
Goose Track
• November
Hearts and Diamonds
in Applique
This and That
• December
Irish Chain

1945
• January

A Heartland Album

Gate or "H" Quilt
Oklahoma Star
• February
Diamonds and Arrow Points
• March
Morning Sun
Southern Star
• April
Scottish Cross
• May
Friendship Quilt
Parallelogram Block
• June
Log Cabin
Grandmother's Cross
• July
Little Wedding Ring
Diversion Quilt
• August
Four Diamonds
Arkansas Traveler
Field Flower Applique
• September
Quilt Mosaic
Modern Envelope
• October
Baby Fan Applique
Circle in a Frame
• November
Small Triangle
Sailboat in Blue and White
Dove at the Window

1946
• February
Fenced-In Star
Cup and Saucer
• March
Simplicity's Delight
• April
Double Irish Chain
Wee Fan
Basket of Bright Flowers
• May
Basket
• July
Semi-Circle Saw
Meadow Rose
Steps to the Altar
• August
White Cross
May Basket for Applique
• October

Return of the Swallows
• November
Rose Dream
• December
Mother's Choice

1947
• January
Red Cross
• February
Springtime Blossoms
• March
Ratchet Wheel
• April
Airplane Motif
Little Boy's Britches
Pieced Sunflower
• June
Road to Oklahoma
Mystery Snowball
Hen and Her Chicks
Tulip Quilt
• July
Four-Leaf Clover
Wedding Ring
• August
Friendship Quilt
Cottage Tulips
• September
May Basket in Floral Tones
Century-Old Tulip Pattern
• October
Frame with Diamonds
Compass Quilt
Builder's Blocks
• November
Carrie Nation
• December
Broken Star
Double "T"
Christmas Star

1948
• January
Steps to the Altar
Crazy Tile
4-Part Strip Block
• February
Circle Upon Circle
Stepping Stones
• March
Wagon Wheels
Boutonniere

• April
Spider Web
Liberty Star
Spring Beauty
• June
Spool Quilt
Royal Diamonds
• July
Double Irish Chain
Sea Shell
• August
Milkmaid's Star
Fans and a Ring
Thrifty Wife
• September
Pig Pen
Log Cabin
• October
Arkansas Star
Old Spanish Tile
• November
Grandmother's Quilt
Whirling Diamonds
• December
Three-In-One
Star Chain
Granny's Choice

1949
• January
Crown of Thorns
Betty's Delight
Tulip Pattern in High
Colors
• February
Long Nine Patch
• March
Autograph Quilt
North Star
Lace Edge
• April
Flash of Diamonds
Terrapin
• May
Magnolia Bud
Kansas Star
• June
Crazy Anne
Chips and Whetstones
• September
Hollows and Squares
Bright Jewel
• October

Gay Dutch Tile
Greek Cross
Ducklings for Friendship
Arrowhead Star
• November
Pussy in the Corner

1950
• January
Broken Stone
• February
Love in a Tangle
Bleeding Heart
Missouri Morning Star
Queen Charlotte's Crown
• March
Snowball
• April
Grandma's Hopscotch
Triangles and Squares
• May
Jewel Quilt
Wishing Ring
• June
Oklahoma String
Scottie Quilt for Boys
• July
Whirligig
• August
Little Girl's Star
Yellow Square
• September
Rainbow Quilt
• October
Parquetry for a Quilt Block
• November
Christmas Tree
Feather-Bone Block
• December
Spindles and Stripes

1951
• January
Little Wedding Ring
• February
Picture Frames
• March
Box of Tulips
Remnant Ovals
Star in a Square
Four Vases
• April

Heirloom Jewel
- May
  Flower Garden
  Mother's Choice
- June
  Soldier Boy
- July
  4-Square Block with
      Diamonds
  Heart for Applique
- September
  Panel of Roses
  Whirling Windmill
- October
  Block of Many Triangles
  Name is Hesper
- December
  Spool Quilt
  Brave Sunflower

1952
- January
  Winged Four-Patch
- March
  Golden Wedding Ring
  Pickle Dish
- April
  My Little Girl's Skirt
  Broken Dish
- May
  Applique in Fruit
- June
  Wagon Wheels Carry
      Me Home
- July
  Star of Four Points
  Rose for Elsa's Pride
- August
  Design for Patriotism
  My Mother's Apron
- September
  Block of Many Triangles
  Triangles and Squares
- November
  Wheel of Fortune
- December
  Broken Circle

1953
- January
  Log Cabin
  Swords and Plowshares
- February

Double Square
- April
  Patty's Summer Parasol
  8-Point Snowflake
- May
  Multiple Square Quilt
- June
  Snowflake Continuity
  Signature Friendship Quilt
  Sea Shells on the Beach
- July
  Basket-Weave
  Friendship Block
  Four Winds
- August
  Pin Wheel
- September
  Sapphire Quilt Block
- October
  Double Irish Chain
- November
  Blazing Star
- December
  Builder's Blocks

1954
- January
  Picket Fence
  Star Garden
- February
  Signature Quilt
  Dragon Fly
- March
  Crystal Star
- May
  Rosebuds of Spring
- June
  Dessert Plate
  Circle Saw
- July
  Greek Cross
  Thousand Stars
- September
  Eight Points in a Square
- November
  Windmill Blades

1955
- January
  Squares and Triangles
  Valentine Quilt
- February
  Wedding Ring

- March
  My Country, For Loyalty
- April
  Journey to California
  Pointed Ovals
- June
  Give This One a Name
- July
  Fool's Square
  Solomon's Temple
  Old-Fashioned Wagon
      Wheel
  Cog Block
- August
  Garden of Flowers
  Many Roads to the
      White House
  Petal Circle in a Square
  Irish Chain Hint
- September
  Name on Each Line
  Moon is New
  Hobby Nook
  Picture Frame
- October
  Scrap Zigzag
- November
  End of the Road
  Cross Patch
  Double Anchor
- December
  Old-Fashioned Goblet
  The Red, the White,
      the Blue
  Roman Stripe
  Old English Wedding Ring

1956
- January
  Nine Patch Star
  Road to Oklahoma
  Puss in the Corner
- February
  Rising Sun
  True America
  Bow Tie in Pink and White
- March
  Monkey Wrench
  Diamond Cluster in a Frame
- April
  Square and Diamonds
  Great Circle
  Quilt for a 4-H Club Room

- May
  Jupiter of Many Points
- June
  Road to Arkansas
  Spearheads and Quarter-
      Circles
  Whirligig for Your Child
- July
  Oklahoma Wonder
  Hands All 'Round
- August
  Orange Peel
  Caps for Witches and
      Dunces
  Star of the West
  Rosette of Points
- September
  Diamonds in the Corners
  Rising Sun
  String Quilt in a Sea Shell
- October
  Pictures in the Stairwell
  Name on Each Friendship
      Block
  Texas or Lone Star
  Design in Geometrics
- November
  Little Wedding Ring
- December
  Old-Fashioned Star Quilt
  Sunburst Quilt
  Necktie

1957
- January
  Quilt Takes Patriotic Hues
- February
  Jewels in a Frame
- April
  Star of Diamond Points
  Oklahoma's Semi-
      Centennial
- May
  Sail Boat
- July
  Soldier at the Window
  Broken Star
- August
  Oil Fields of Oklahoma
- September
  Windmills All Around

- October

A Heartland Album

Oklahoma's Square Dance
• November
  Road to Oklahoma

1958
• January
  Cross is Mother's Choice
• February
  Old-Fashioned Pin Wheel
  Missouri Daisy
• April
  Basket Weave Friendship
    Quilt
• May
  Hicks Flower Basket
• June
  Old Indian Trail
  Ocean Wave of Many Prints
• August
  Scrap Collector's Quilt
  Hour Glass in a New Picture
• September
  Seven Stars
  Dogwood Blossom
  Friendship Block in
    Diamonds
• November
  Flying Colors

1959
• January
  Coverlet in Jewel Tones
• March
  Drunkard's Path
• April
  Old-Fashioned Indian Puzzle
  Wedding Ring
• June
  Spider Web Gone Awry
• July
  6-Point Flower Garden
  Ferris Wheel
• August
  From a Grandmother's
    Collection
• September
  Carnival Time
• October
  Squares and Diamonds
• November
  Space for Many Names
  Yours for Luck
• December

Window of Triangles
Her Sparkling Jewels

1960
• January
  Monkey Wrench
• February
  Turtle Quilt
• March
  Cypress
  Rain Drop
• April
  Narcissus Motif
• May
  Evening Star
  The Rope and Anchor
• June
  Big Bear's Paw
• July
  Friendship Quilt for Many
    Purposes
• August
  Ever Popular Log Cabin
• September
  Bright Morning Star
  Cat's Cradle

1961
• January
  Historic Oak Leaf
  Squares of Diamonds
• February
  Sunflower Motif
• March
  Bell
• April
  Signatures for Golden
    Memories
Spring Beauty
• May
  Little Boy's Breeches
  Fan of Many Colors

2001
• January
  Bittersweet
• February
  Dandelion
• March
  Wood Sorrel
• April
  Sweet William

• May
  Wild Rose
• June
  Wild Cucumber
• July
  Missouri Primrose
• August
  Wild Morning Glory
  Dogwood Blossom
  Hickory Leaf
  Strawberry Basket
  Magnolia Blossom
  Kite
  Puss in Corner
  Bluebell
• September
  Sunflower
• October
  Indian Paintbrush
• November
  Aster
• December
  Johnny-Jump-Up

2002
• January
  Patriotism
• February
  Diversity
• March
  Opportunity
• April
  Community
  Tulip
  Amaryllis
  Poppies
  Fantasy
  Bluebells
  Dahlia
  Dogwood
  Vinca Vine
  Rose Basket
  Wood Daisy
  Sunflower Basket
  Angel Clematis
• May
  Remembrance
• June
  Justice
• July
  Liberty
• August
  Thrift

• September
  Industry
• October
  Humor
• November
  Perseverance
• December
  Charity

Other Kansas City Star Quilt
    Books

Star Quilts I: One Piece at a
    Time
Star Quilts II: More Kansas City
    Star Quilts
Star Quilts III: Outside the Box
Star Quilts IV: The Sister Block
Star Quilts V: Prairie Flower - A
    Year on the Plains
Star Quilts VI: Kansas City
    Quiltmakers
Star Quilts VII: O'Glory -
    Americana Quilt Blocks
    from The Kansas City Star
Star Quilts VIII: Hearts and
    Flowers
Star Quilts IX: Roads and
    Curves Ahead
Star Quilts X: Celebration of
    American Life
Santa's Parade of Nursery
    Rhymes
Fan Quilt Memories

For more information or to
order, call 816-234-4636 and
say "Books." Or visit
www.PickleDish.com